ANCHOR BOOKS

POETS DEBUT

First published in Great Britain in 1995 by
ANCHOR BOOKS
1-2 Wainman Road, Woodston,
Peterborough, PE2 7BU

SB ISBN 1 85930 032 4

Foreword

Anchor Books is a small press, established in 1992, with the aim of promoting readable poetry to as wide an audience as possible.

We hope to establish an outlet for writers of poetry who may have struggled to see their work in print.

The poems presented here have been selected from many entries. Editing proved to be a difficult and daunting task and as the Editor, the final selection was mine.

The poems chosen represent a cross-section of styles and content. They have been sent from all over the world, written by young and old alike, united in the passion for writing poetry.

I trust this selection will delight and please the authors and all those who enjoy reading poetry.

Andrew Head
Editor

CONTENTS

THE DOG KENNELS

There's a lovely spot I know
That's home in many ways,
For little canine friends to spend
Their summer holidays.
They stay there when their owners go
On trips both far and near,
Tho' some, that like the place so much,
Have stayed there for a year!
But come the summer hols. and lo!
The population grows,
To such extent that everywhere
There's rows - and rows - and rows
            of
Dogs in the porchway, dogs on the floor,
Dogs on the ceiling, dogs in ev'ry door,
Dogs who knock you over, dogs who trip you up,
Dogs as large as horses, dogs just like a pup.
Big ones, small ones, whites, blacks and reds,
Dogs in the wardrobe, dogs under beds.
Dogs in the fireplace, dogs up the flue,
Dogs in the dairy, dogs in the loo!
Dogs in the caravan, dogs in the pen,
There's hardly room to wag a tail for
        Sheba and for Ben!

Joe Browne

MY PLACE

On the other side of my window,
There is a place where,
Sometimes, I fly.
Over the concrete building blocks,
Down through the gorge above the river,
Along the motorways of lorries and cars,
Each moving their own separate lives within.
Across the fields of snow,
And the forests,
Rich in green and brown and sounds and life.
Above the scaffolds of creation, renovation and destruction,
And the silent cemetery,
To the mountains, walls of time.
I return softly, through the peaceful sky.
To my window, high in its own concrete tower,
To fly again tomorrow,
In this place none other can match.
For this is my home.
All that I see,
On the other side of my window.

Amelia McKnight

LOVERS

Come with me my darling to a
    Bed of silk and lace.
Then let us take each other
    To another time and place.
We'll love as only lovers do -
    Chase dreams across the sky,
On a wondrous pure white
    Stallion - with wings so we can fly!

L M Walford

UNTITLED

You never said you'd found her
That girl who took you away
How was I supposed to know
You weren't gonna stay
But after a while guessing was easy
When you know some one well
You know what to look for
You know how to tell
But still you never told me
That you wanted out
You let me go on thinking
And living in doubt
I don't know what she looks like
Your replacement for me
I've never seen you with her
In the car or on the street
You come around to see me
But only when you can
You don't come as often
You stick to a plan
You only seem to want me
When she's not around
But because I love you
I'm always easily found
Take my word for it though
One day you'll search the whole world through
And when you come to find me
I'll be stuck to some one else - just like you.

Elaine Reynolds

POEM FOR BRIDGET

Through suffering yourself
You learnt compassion for others
Your understanding goes beyond the words that are spoken
You see the sadness and despair for the dreams that are broken
Through your midnight velvet eyes
You communicate with me

Through your gaze you allow me to be free
But when you are gone the haunting memories come flooding back
I'm on the defensive, lonely and waiting for the attack
Of long years to envelop my thoughts and crowd my brain
Bringing me down and leaving me shattered once again.

They say that time is a healer
And in the end I shall mend
When and if I become my whole self
Most of the thanks will be to you, Bridget, my friend.

Kim Harrison

BALLOONING

From your worries, you want to get away
Then hire a balloon for the day
It's a bit of a struggle to get inside
But then you are in for a marvellous ride
Float over the houses, and trees so tall
Look at the people, don't they look small
Wonderful view and not a sound
Even from all the traffic on the ground
Oh what peace, and what bliss,
If only, all the world could be like this

Brenda Day

GOLDCREST IN THE SNOW

We found you lying in the snow
The *cause of death* we'll never know
Tiny bird so perfectly made
Lying dead in a woodland glade.
Why did you die? You sweet little thing
With golden head and tiny wing
Was it lack of food that proved too much
Or the bitter cold the *final touch*?
What a pity you'll never see the spring
Bring warmth and your mate and a song to sing
Never again to fly and build your clever nest
Just silent! Death has brought you rest.
And when we walk this way again
We'll listen for your call - but all in vain.
Tiny, tiny little bird
Never again will your song be heard.

Christine Darlow

THE MOON AND STARS

I wonder why the moon's so high
   The stars so shining bright
I ponder and I wonder why
   This world's a lovely sight

I wonder why the lovely flowers
   Cheer us the way they do
I wonder why some lonely hours
   Are filled with wonder too

I wonder why God put us here
   It's just a wonder too
I wonder why he seems so near
   When everything looks blue

R Brawn

TEAM WORK

There's this team of three, who you can see every day,
They are the best that you'll find, it's just their way,
Who needs to shop at the local big store?
When they greet you so well, as you come through the door,
The name of the shop is *Crown Road Stores*,
You'll see *Reg* there, when he opens the doors,
Reg is the boss, or so I've been told,
At fifty eight years young, he's not very old,
Reg opens at six, always wide awake,
In through the door, comes this chap called *Jake*,
He heads for the fridge, a can of special brew,
Why *Reg* can you spare me a fag or two?
Sandra glides through the door, the time is eight,
Another minute more, then she'd have been late,
Tall and slender, with short grey hair,
Scottish I think, 'cause her accent's not clear,
On goes the kettle, she's making some tea,
Morning shouts *Reg,* can you make one for me?
Ham to slice, and rolls have yet to be made,
Take lots of money, then you'll surely get paid,
Clare's in at nine, there's the shelves to fill,
Spuds to weight up, while working the till,
Friendly staff, always a smile on their face,
Shop in this store, you're in the right place,
It's been great to work, with you happy folk,
'Cause there's always time left, for a laugh and a joke,
At the end of the season, hope I don't get the sack,
For I'd like to think, you'll let me come back,
Would like to help out, if someone is sick,
Just give me a call, I'll be there in a tick.

Chris Edwards

GARDEN IN THE RAIN

Lincoln, beryl, olivine,
Sage and willow, emerald green,
Every green you've ever seen,
Garden in the rain.

Ruby-glowing, coral, wine,
Crimson, scarlet, flowers of mine,
Every red you could divine,
Garden in the rain.

Azure, sapphire, ultramarine,
Bluebells sway and cornflowers lean,
Every blue you've ever seen,
Garden in the rain.

Gold and topaz, daffodil,
Buttercup and primrose frill,
Every yellow you could will,
Garden in the rain.

Snowy-gleaming, ivory-bright,
Alabaster, creamy-white,
In every white you can delight,
Garden in the rain.

Slug and snail and centipede,
Greenfly, blackfly, creeping weed,
Every pest you never need,
Garden in the rain.

Daphne Goddard

KILLING ANGELS

I dreamed I saw the Holy Man
A sit a seat on high
Fine robes adorned his girded loin
A glint a-gleamed his eye
And thunder raged and lightning flashed
As trembled voice said I
'I have to question you, my Lord,
Why do the animals die?'

I love the lambs in green field play
The ponies down they lie
The goats they graze their days away
Their young for milk they cry
And cows caress their little ones
Below the big blue sky
I have to ask again, my Lord,
Why do the animals die?

Men fight battles o'er the seas
The land and in the sky
They thrust and parry, smite and slay
And kill with whom they vie
They sit a-stride their foaming charge
A sword held way up high
Ne'er once they ask of you, my Lord,
Why do the animals die?

Why is it that you take their love
And give them no reply
To bleated braying helplessness
From couped-up pens and sty
Why can't you see the hurt and pain
That lingers in their eye
As death cuts short their strangled cry
'Why do I have to die
My Lord,
Why *do* I have to die?

Paul Gidman

SPEND THE NIGHT

Oh, so I'm to spend the night?
You've got it all *nice* and right?
Sweet music of course, and soft words
with no protest to be made or heard?
Dimmer switches and candlelight,
with no need to fake a fight?

Soft pillows in a comfortable bed,
satin sheets in an oh so subtle red?
Going through the usual motions
with, of course, the usual precautions?
A timed crescendo with perfected growl?
Extra toothbrush and a clean towel?
Late start at work tomorrow,
no regrets and no sorrow?

Cute, clever little seduction scene.
Oh, mister, I can see where you've been.
Oh, yes, you're f ***ing right,
I'm to spend the night.

J F Griffin

THE LOTTERY

It's lottery time as we all fantasise
Millions of pounds, that elusive first prize
Down to the shops with a pound in my hand
Dreaming of ships and a foreign land
My numbers the same, all picked with great care
Birthdays and ages of mum, dad and aunt clare
Three numbers, that's all, gets you £10.00 of loot
Not one of mine yet, has appeared in that shoot
Now what if I won all six million quid
I'd give some to mum, our dad and our kid.
No work any more, tell the boss I've retired
Perhaps buy the company, tell him he's been fired
Buy lots of clothes and a luxury car
Mortgage paid up free drinks at the bar
Holiday time to Disney Land
Trips round the world not previously planned
Brand new house a flat in New York
New friends that once nodded and now want to talk
But now it's all over that fantasy flight
It's five past eight on Saturday night.

T Lappage

SPEAKING OUT FOR FERALS

They say we're dangerous
They say we're wild
Better watch your neighbours
Better watch that child

Have you ever seen us, well have you?
Hiding in the shadows as we pass through
It's all very silly, really you see
Timid and shy, by nature are we

Those who know will understand
We're not dangerous or wild
We're just very wary
Of you and that child

So leave us alone
Let us be on our way
To live our lives
The traditional way!

Samantha Kerr

BLACKBERRY PICKING

I always go blackberry picking round early September
With friends, jars, cans, drinks and all that, you remember?
Walking through fields, through lanes and forts.
Where it's creepy at night, even day that sort.
The sort where luminous flowers grow and glow,
And the birds sing in the high trees where the violent wind doth blow.
The day is getting on and we are full of bruises and stings,
Still cold, still wet that's what September brings.
Looks around nothing there, then my friend says 'There's a big one up
                                                                    here!'
We all run to see, look there's one here too, and here, and there.
She stretches out to get it not knowing what will happen,
She's got it we cried then she fell, I suppose it had to happen.
We begin to fill our jars and cans,
And nothing but prickles all over our hands.
At last we've filled our jars and cans full of blackberries,
Very little are green, most are purple and others are red as cherries.
Now we go home all soaking wet, wellingtons full of grass,
And now, before long, September will pass.

Sheila J Witts (13)

11

SOMEONE

It's good to have someone that you can talk to
And tell all the things that are worrying you.
You can cry in front of and feel no shame -
Who you know will always treat you the same,
No matter what you say and do,
They will always be there, for you.
Who calms you down when you are mad
And thinks of you when you are sad,
With whom you can discuss your fears
And occasionally, will share your tears.
Who you could ring both day and night
And wouldn't laugh, like others might.
Someone who'll be there, through and through.
I have someone . . . do you?

Vicky Clarke

TRANSFORMATION SCENE

'Twas early morn, there seemed to be
No line between grey sky and sea.
The little girl ran down to meet
The waves, they frilled her naked feet.

She said, I wish that I could play
Like you, all through the summer's day,
The waves replied, we are not free,
But fettered to the mighty sea.

They told me that the sea was blue
But now I know that is not true.
So said the disappointed child.
The sun rose, and all nature smiled.

She gazed, entranced, the sea the skies,
Were changed to blue, before her eyes.

Pauline Ransley

TILL DEATH US DO PART

The baby seal snuggles close to his mother
He sleeps as he feels the warmth of each other
Snow is falling outside their warm lair
They lay close together without a care
It's so peaceful and quiet, not a care in the world
they both sleep, it's so quiet you can't hear a word,
the pup wakes in the morning and goes out to play
It's the beginning of a beautiful day
Mother waits for her child full of delight
Playing in the snow, brilliant, white
Suddenly there are footsteps crunching in snow
She hides quietly hoping they'll go
there are two men coming towards her
She is overcome with fear, they want her fur
they are holding clubs which are dripping blood
One lands beside her with an almighty thud
She thinks of her pup and fears for his life
Suddenly she is stabbed with a very sharp knife
A club crushes her scull as it lands on her head
Her fur is taken, the mother is dead
the pup returns waiting for food
there lays his mothers covered in blood
A tear forms in the little one's eye
He's left all alone, why did she die
For the sake of some fur which is had by these men
When will it stop? I want to know, when,
the pup lays by his mother, waiting for her to wake
Let's stop this slaughter, just for his sake.

Anna Hocking

HOW MUCH DOES THE CAGED BIRD NEED THE FREEDOM OF FLIGHT?

I still have my head, so to speak and
to a limited extent, during periods of humility
to see and to hear.
I still have my limbs,
Two arms, positioned neatly . . . for strategy,
and two equally strategic legs
for following in my father's footsteps,
but mainly for pacing.
I still have all the necessary organs, that is
if you can accept the utilitarian definition of
for example, *The Heart*.
i.e. A hollow muscular organ, which by rhythmic contraction
and relaxation, drives the blood around the vascular system.
. . . But am I intact?
I lack a soul, that elusive entity,
cherished by Methodists and eagerly sought
by demons and mystics alike.
But despite the dedication and objective censure
of modern science, this quantity remains hidden.
I find myself wondering, during my most reflective moments
'How much do I need one?'
About as much as a caged bird needs the freedom of flight . . .

P Davies Thomas

ONE WORLD?

One world? - No there are many,
We each have a world of our own
The outer one is for all to share,
The inner . . . is ours alone.

Here, we can mould and colour,
Adjust the light and shade,
With one thought, can re-arrange
The sanctuary we have made.

Here, to create such inner peace,
It is possible to hear.
Music in the silence,
Exquisite - crystal clear.

Here, no-one else can enter
Unless invited, for
Without an invitation,
There can never be a door!

Delia Adcock

SPRING

Tulips - resplendent in yellow and red
Standing so straight in their earthly bed
Woodlands of celandines wind flowers green trees
Grass in the fields - on the hill and the lea
Daffodils - golden like the sun
Shining so brightly - spring has begun
Dancing and swaying in the breeze, *so trim*
White narcissi, perfumed ladies prim.
Shy young snowdrops - violets demure
Crocus, birds peck their nectar for sure
All these bright flowers appear in spring.
Bringing us hope, we surely should sing.

E Phillips

THE COMPLETE MAN

That mild and melancholy figure
Who rests contented with his lot,
Waiting for life to come to him,
Mocking those who choose to try.

He fidgets uncomfortably, alone,
His eloquence and magnetism wasted.
Despite himself, he reaches out to
The Complete Man stirring within.

This new Man makes play of life;
Obstacles are there to be hurdled,
Not to be discussed and mused over
In a dimly lit drawing room.

He walks confidently out of the haze,
His melancholy disguised with ease,
Looking at life as someone who lives
Not as a figure contemplating death.

The Complete Man will not waver,
For he is fuelled by the passion
Which had always been lurking
Beneath that melancholy exterior.

When he is alone he will reflect
And the mild and melancholy one
Will assess The Complete Man,
Then retire, content at last.

Lawrence Hurley

JOURNEY TO HEAVEN

The night was cold and dark and bleak
As I walked down this tiny street.
People strolled past shop and alley
But not a person would stop and dally
So on I walked with thoughts depressed
Until I came to this house addressed
'Welcome, welcome, all ye who walk alone
And make this house just like your own.'
So in I walked with trembling feet
And left the cold and dismal street
Into this house, so friendly and warm
At once my thoughts changed, like a storm
And before me came a vision of light
An angel clothed in silk and white
Stretched out her long and slender arms
And beckoned me with a voice so calm
Into her arms I slowly went
From this bitter world to a land of content.

Pam Fitzjohn

DANIEL

You bring me laughter, you're my pride and joy,
I love you very much my boy.
I know sometimes, I make you cry,
For reasons that, you don't know why.
I take you home, we're at the door,
That my heart hurts, you can be sure.
But remember that no matter what,
I'll come running, like a shot.
And when you need me, I'll be there,
I promise you, I'll always care.

C A Haas

DESTINY

Destiny is our path through life
Daily, we encounter, trouble and strife
Also joy, happiness, tears and sorrow
Never knowing what we'll meet tomorrow.

Our journey starts in our mother's womb
Finishes as we enter our final tomb
Between these points is a long, long road
Along which we travel, bearing a heavy load.

Of responsibility to ourselves and each other
More, especially, to our father and mother
Who welcomed us with love and joy
No matter be we girl or boy.

As we enter life's last mile
Let us do so with a happy smile
With endless joy within our heart
As, from this life, we prepare to depart.

C Ellaby

HOME COMFORTS

Today,
I bought a bar of chocolate,
I took a bite,
remembered . . .
I took another,
   then another,
      then another.

I'd better buy another tomorrow
maybe it'll help me forget.

C A Umney

LETTING GO

The time is arriving for my baby to leave,
Don't laugh at me please just let me grieve,
I know he's all grown up a big boy you'll say,
Alright I know! he's turned 18 today.

The memories come flooding back into my mind,
Of when he was a young one so thoughtful and kind,
Then a shadow appears do you know what that means,
Yes, you've guessed it he's come to his teens.

Oh! the rows and the cheeking I can't take much more,
The times I'm so tempted to show him the door,
We've got our own personal Jekyll and Hyde,
I'm beginning to think that he never died.

Have you see this phone bill we hear his dad say,
He must have been on it every minute of the day,
Wait till he's moved into a home of his own,
He'll know the expense when he's got his own phone.

The music pounds out boom di di boom,
The ornaments shaking all over the room,
I try to ignore it we were all young long ago,
But what happened to Cliff, Elvis or Matt Monro.

I know he's a headache but the good points are there,
He needs me most definitely when he can't do his hair,
All he's got to do is give me that smile,
And all of his bad points disappear for a while.

Well tomorrow is here and I can't say I'm glad,
I'll miss him so terribly and so will his dad,
For all his wrong doings he's a good boy at heart,
Well he's got to be hasn't he because of us he's a part.

S Baker

FRIGHTENED

Frightened of death, frightened I'll die,
The car tumbled over,
And ripped Shona's eye.
Shona was in hysterics, couldn't calm her down
She was lying on the grass face straight down.
I thought she was dead,
Couldn't bear to look,
A few cars stopped to take a look.
The policeman came.
I didn't know what to say,
He asked me questions along the way.
Got to the hospital,
Shona was wheeled in.
I heard her screaming, when they were stitching her up.
I wish it was me, who got stitched up,
A typical male got off with a cut.
He was discharged, I was kept in.
Haven't seen Shona for about two days.
I hope she's alright, everyone prays.
Frightened of death, frightened I'll die.
Frightened of all this, I wish I could cry.
Shona had an operation on her head.
The three of us were lucky
We were not dead.
I'm so relieved, that she's O K.
Maybe she'll get out tomorrow
Or the next day.

Leeann Johnston

FOUR MEN

There have been four men in my life
To one, a daughter, then daughter-in-law, mother and then wife.
The first, my father, wrote verses to me
They were left on the sideboard each morning to see.

My father-in-law, he wrote many a book
And when they were published he gave me a look.
He wrote poems and verses both happy and sad
And now he has gone of these works I am glad.

My son, doesn't like verse, doesn't like it at all.
He is a car salesman so tells stories that are tall.
He can't write a novel, but, tells quite a tale
That's why as a salesman he never will fail.

My husband, the singer who will sing any song
He also will try to right anything wrong
He's Cliff and he's Elvis, he could even be Bing.
But all that he wants is a song he can sing!

Margaret Etherington

WHO AM I

I can hear the shadows playing
On the distant shore
I can see time, moving slowly
Across the ocean floor
I can breathe the winds of change -
Hold them in my hand
I can ride the crystal meteors
In their unknown land
I can sail the boat of fortune
Down the river fate
And I can fly the clouds of love
And swim the sea of hate.

M T Bridge

WOOD OF DEPRIVATION

I am fighting back the branches of decay,
as I stumble through the wood of deprivation.
The ground has soured beneath me,
the earth crumbles with every foreboding step.

My loss is reflected by my surroundings,
amongst the cracking of dead twigs;
I must live till death engulfs my humble shell.

I must be reminded of my loss by the landscape,
which lived when I lived,
flourished with joy when my life knew meaning,
and dies with me;
as my life loses meaning with every passing hour.

My life and surroundings are colourless,
the joy has been lost with my faith in happiness,
the birds are no longer a part of my life,
I fail to hear their songs,
see the growing of flowers,
or rejoice in their colours and aromas.

My body fails to function with meaning,
merely with necessity.

The decay grows greater,
and the loss of life around me,
increases as time passes.
My senses turn inside,
it's the only direction left
for a loveless existence.

Despair has struck,
my wood has died.
The many branches are broken
and have fallen upon the pale, lifeless soil.

S Westmore

THE RIVER

Oh to be by the river
At this time of year
Gently ripping murmuring
Whispering in my ear

Trickling dancing shining
As onward it doth go
Reflecting precious sunlight
As down its path it flow

Too soon that gentle river
Change as it goes by
Bending rush and flowers
Beneath the silvery sky

On and on in madness
By its banks it flows
Crashing mighty waters
Thundering as it goes.

Where, or where are you going
Pressing on still more
You, once a gentle river
Beneath the ocean floor

O my gentle river
Once I thee adored
That life I had by the river
Alas I see no more.

W Frary

MELANIE

No little friend this weekend
With Toni's paper letter send
To this little artist and DJ
At very latest Friday next will see

At church hall she will make the show
With a little help from UNC you know
But perhaps she'll ring before this date
When chip and gravy make bedtime late

Sharon phoned this morning asking when
That the junior disco starts again
To her I said one night we'd meet
With drink guess what and chips to eat

Toni and Paul for two days have gone away
Must first ask Toni what she has to say
Whose ideas are best to fill the spot
It's Melanie that I love a lot

Sharon though for long I've known
During which time my love has grown
Two great girls it would appear I've got
The best to choose for this top spot

Though lots of help I often need
Be it dancing singing or just to feed
No envelopes, air mail this will have to Melanie go
Just room in Huxley Street to land ho ho.

Bryan Dearden

MY JO'BURG CHRISTMAS TREE

The sweetest spot in all the world for ever it shall be
My dear old home in Jo'burg Town with a Jacaranda tree
And though I'm many miles away in a land across the sea
My heart is there in that land so fair, by a Jacaranda tree.

For years and years you've given shade and beauty to our land
Pre-Christmas decorations untouched by human hand
No flashing lights or tinsel can e'er provide for me
The Christmas decorations of my Jacaranda tree.

Each Christmas morn, a crib we placed, and Christmas carols sang
And 'neath your shade a table laid as happy voices rang
No holly or not mistletoe can e'er provide for me
The Christmas decorations of my Jacaranda tree.

How I miss that glorious sunshine, and when evening shadows fall
The calling of the crickets 'neath a rambling old stone wall
In moonlight on a summer's night your shadows still I see
Oh, I'll ne'er forget the beauty of my Jacaranda tree.

And so dear Jo'burg town I send my greetings from afar
Ariding through the moonlight on my lonely Christmas star
Awinging like the swallows from a land far o'er the sea
To my dear old home in Jo'burg town by a Jacaranda tree.

E Larkin

THE SILENCE

8.38 - The cannon fires
And one hundred thousand people rise to their feet
To honour their dead
They turn their eyes to the sky
To meet the gaze of a thousand heroes
And for two minutes Heaven and Earth unite
In solemn remembrance.

Kate Ellis

NOSTALGIA

Little lady by the fire
She was eighty yesterday
Friends relations just a memory
Years ago they went away

By the forest in the valley
Near the sound of bubbling streams
Faded photos in an album
Bringing back a million dreams

Wads of letters hiding secrets
Neatly wrapped with rubber bands
Such an effort trying to read them
Failing sight and trembling hands

As she wraps her shawl around her
Tries in vain to beat the cold
Feebly wipes away a teardrop
It's not my fault that I am old

Dying embers in the fireplace
Slowly burn away and die
Then she heard a voice from heaven
It was her calling from the sky

Alan Taylor

STANSTED AIRPORT

We'll build an airport here they say
Waving a languid hand,
Destroying the work of a thousand years
In a rich and fertile land.

We'll build an airport here they say
Ignoring the bitter tears
For homes destroyed and future wrecked,
We want the land, who cares?

Shattered the peace when the moon is high
And the badgers creep from their sett,
Instead of a wide and silent sky
The howling scream of a jet.

The oak trees down beside the ride,
The fields where lovers stray,
They'll devastate the countryside
Bulldoze the woods away.

In this beloved land of ours
It's here we want to stay,
With a stroke of a pen, those London men
Bulldoze our lives away.

Freda Burton

SMALL COMFORT

She feels no pain, her bruises press, on furry face so warm
Is where she finds her comfort, lest the adults do more harm.
No bloodline links their love so meek, her parents cannot give.
Which moves wet salt on fevered cheek for a soul that longs to live.

Hot fishy breath she will not reject, this warmth is more than none.
This feline charm gains more respect than where her life came from.
To love, to smell, warm sun-kissed fur can bring some small respite.
To feel on fingers velvet purr, turns darkness into light.

Sheila Evans

MY COUNTRY GARDEN

It's not found in a gardeners' book
because of a wild and overgrown look
Nothing planned as town people do
there is no time to see it through.
Weather and nature are ruling the spread
before finding time the weeds are overhead.
beneath the flourishing wild confusion
planting seedling smothered by the intrusion
Buttercups are common - may be
so are the little white daisy.
As dandelions with pinks entwine
all get blessed by the sun that shines.
Oh why bother, let nature take its course
like broom so yellow and gold the common gorse.
Are just as pretty to the eyes
in my country garden under the sky . . .

Maja Padgett

THE WONDERS OF LIFE

As old age creeps on,
I sit all alone,
I have time on my hands,
To sit and ponder,
Life to me is still,
A great wonder.

People look at me,
As if I have never lived,
The body lets me down,
The spirit still,
Has so much to give.

I was once young,
And so full of life.
I have lived through,
Toil and strife.

Now I sit, silent and still,
And live on my memories,
Which I can recall at my will,
So sad I am not,
Life is a wonder.
So on those thoughts,
I now must ponder.

Wendy Forni

ONCE UPON A RAIN FOREST

The rain falls cleaning the air,
leaving it fresh without despair,
Soaking into the dry cracked ground,
to swell the seeds of life rotund.

The earth replenished sighs content,
New life groans with back bent,
forces upward to break free,
into a forest without a tree.

For awhile it stands on its own,
as if the only seed ever sown,
lost in the emptiness of a land,
that's been destroyed by man's own hand.

Soon it's joined by more and more,
the natural balance beginning to restore.
The rain falls through the trees down into the fern,
breathing life into the world again so that
mankind can live and learn?

Kevin Dent

LOCH NESS MONSTER

Where is that Loch Ness Monster that people want to see
She is not any old tiddler that you fish from the Dee
Nessie is quite famous been heard of far and wide
And her picture front page cover in a glossy tourist guide.

Early every summer a sighting is foreseen
And all the roads get blocked right to *Aberdeen*
They come from many countries flying round the globe
To get one glimpse of *Nessie* would *fairly be the job*

High Tec cameras binoculars round their necks
Underwater lenses that pick up tiny specks
Americans Aussies Canadians and quite a lot of Japs
They keep coming back Inverness is on the map.

The town is kept busy hotels do a roaring trade
And lads with hiring boats think a fortune will be made
Trips up and down the water several every hour
Queues of tourists waiting often caught up in a shower

Does Nessie really try to hide deep below the sea
A creature most elusive to the likes of you and me
Does she want her life kept private or does she want a mate
They try down bits and pieces just really monster bait

There has been several sightings a snap or two for proof
A humpy backed scaly form with a body as big as a house
I don't want to meet her on a dark and lonely night
Because I really am a coward and she'd give me a fright.

Her beauty sleep she should be having when there is a new full moon
Getting ready for her season she is a tourist boon
I hope they never catch her with their supersonic jets
Fish and chips can be rather nice but who wants *Nessie on a plate.*

Rosemary Peter

THE BELL

In Africa's sunny climate
Where I served in Company C
They made me a company runner
And a bike they gave to me
Across the plains I pushed the thing
And over the mountain peaks
With never a blooming road in sight
This really angered me
We crept through mountain passes
Behind the enemy lines
And every time I hit a rut
The flaming bell rang out
It was later I learned from the Germans
While reclining in Stalag 4G
That half of Rommel's Panzers
Had been silent, just listening for me
They knew exactly where we were
By the sound of my bicycle bell
And the days of the Company
Runner were over for ever

Just because of a bell.

George Kitchen

UNTITLED

Gnawing gnawing gnawing inside
What is happening to my mind
Anger hurt terror fear
Eyes always brimming with tears.
What's wrong am I going mad
Or just heartbroken and very sad
My heart is broken it will never mend
To hurt like this must be the end

Mary McBride

THE RIVER

The river rippled gently through fields of green
Occasionally a whirlpool was to be seen
It settled again and flowing onward ran
Through rocks then dashed against banks and began
Gathering speed like clouds pushed by a force
Its once calm song very angry grew on a course
Of dark destruction. Sweeping without remorse
Relentless in the chase to end its life and
Yet knowing. Some small part will band
Together and unite the flow unstoppable once more.
So on it raged sweeping trees and all before.
Faster it went down hill and dale, into street,
House and shop. Taking all before it straight
Into all the fury that it could generate.
It tossed all in its path, this way and that
Racing and swirling in mad abandon
Overflowing where it could at random.
Then slowly, so slowly, it changed its pace
Now at the end of its long chase,
It ran lightly, and calmly, now almost content
The energy and rage, at long last spent.

E P Devereux

MONTY

I bumped into a python,
I said how do you do?
It seemed his name was Monty,
He'd just come from the zoo.

His skin was quite amazing,
A technicolour dream,
But when he tried to squeeze me,
I began to scream.

Now Monty, you must let me go
Or else I'll have to choose
Do I want a snakeskin bag,
A belt or even shoes?

Now we are the best of friends
For Monty is my pet,
He knows he must behave himself
Or it's *off to the vet*

Annette Connolly

THE OLD TRACK

Thirty years ago, they closed the line,
Took up the rails and most officially banished
The engines puffing up the long incline.
The sleepers vanished,
Dying in flames at night, on cottage hearths.
Silence settled where the trains had run,
Men, for their travel, followed other paths,
The way seemed gone.
Little we thought to see it live again -
We reckoned without nature's healing work.
The ravaged track became a grass grown lane
Where pheasants lurk.
Cradled by hedges, warm against the breeze,
Bedded in shady woods and sunny banks,
Bird song in spring, in summer loud with bees,
Trees in untidy ranks.

But sometimes, wandering dreamy down that lane,
I still hear echoes of a ghostly train.

Patricia Taylor

AT THE FALL

Sweetly the Autumn days glide slowly by
    Like nectar from some fairy spring:
Leaves sere and yellow, multi-veined and quite crisp,
    Fall softly as an angelic wing.

Massed foliage on hillside, green brown and gold,
    Lie sun-kissed, benign, serene;
The earth, sea and sky, as ever distilling
    Their beauty and charm the glad heart fulfilling

Handsome the honey bee, red-banded and furred,
    A-rifling the flowers of their sweet-scented food,
Then staggering, inebriated and dazed,
    Back to its workshop deep down in the wood.

As the shortened day dawns, fine veils of grey mist
    Drape the gaunt limbs of the shadowy trees;
Then sharp, sudden frosts as the evening descends
    Diamantle the earth in a picturesque frieze.

The Autumn sun sets, so gradual and slow,
    'Neath the half circle rim at the edge of the globe,
Garlanded, iridescent, in rainbowesque hues,
    Reflecting the radiance of Heaven's jewelled robe.

Oh, twilight, stay with us just for a while,
    One glorious hour more, the last, loving mile;
Stay with the last moments, keep open the door,
    Moments to give thanks, to kneel and adore.

D Coull

FRANCE 1915

We won a hundred yards today,
Through mud and slime, through cutting fire.
We lost some men,
But still,
We won a hundred yards today.

We won a hundred yards today.
The dawn attack was no surprise.
They knew we'd come.
And yet
We won a hundred yards today.

We won a hundred yards today.
The generals said we'd turn the war
By sacrifice.
And so
We won a hundred yards today.

We won a hundred yards today.
We took the ridge. But they attacked
To push us back.
At first
We won a hundred yards today.

We lost a hundred yards today.
For gas and shells, the murderous hail,
We were no match
At all.
We lost a hundred yards today.

We lost a hundred yards today.
Embittered, bloody, to our holes,
Stumbling heroes,
So few.
We lost a thousand men today.

Alan F Hunter

GOD'S MIRACLE

When God made the world
He took seven days
Six he did work
The seventh he did say
There's something not right
But what could it be
I'll look in my pot
And see what I see
He took his great pot
And into it threw
Some blue from the sky
Some golden sun too
A sprinkle of star dust
The rose bud's perfume
The angels gave love
As they danced round the room
With a small piece of rainbow
God stirred with great might
As all God's small creatures
Sighed with delight
With a few drops of honey
He gave one last twirl
And there in the pot
Lay a small baby girl

E Balkwill

ICE

An opaque moon
holds centre stage
and heralds the coming of ice.

Few escape from this visiting omnipresence
which metaphorphosises moisture
creating an agglomeration
of temporary shapes and patterns.

The land surrenders
to another change in texture
and bears the fossil-like imprints of its latest visitors
with fortitude.

The victor plays his silent rhapsody
across a scale of octaves
whilst Paris waits silently
in the person of the sun.

Glenn K Murphy

THE ONLY FOUR X FOUR X FAR

There's rain falling over withering heights,
as the free reining equine delights,
follow the furrow till the fading light,
has drained their failing might.

Setting their sights to view,
down an autumnal avenue,
to five rails debarring the way,
in misty moss embarking decay.

Drawn with a dragging sound,
engraving a groove in the ground,
to notes forged on fluted lines,
that are hammered out in harmonic times.

Paul Banos

UNTITLED

We have just bought a Golden Crown
And we think it is the best in town
It has the biggest bed we've ever seen
And the end washroom, oh what a dream.

We have never owned a tourer before
But so far we love it more and more
We plan to tour England and Wales
Enjoying the hills, and rivers, and dales.

We may visit Scotland one fine day
That's if we are able to find our way.
The Yorkshire Dales, we can't wait to try
That's why our caravan is a great buy.

With the Volvo and tourer off we go,
Not too fast, and not too slow
Not too heavy, and not to light
Checking the nose-weight is just right.

C Evans

TRIBUTE TO JOHN BETJEMAN

They laid to rest a Cornishman,
A man of prose and verse,
Words of wit and wisdom,
Love truth and mirth.

There are but few, who can find the words,
To philosophically reason why,
He who was full of eloquence,
Found them for the shy.

On great and small occasions,
With ink he set his seal,
Divining in man's most innermost thoughts,
A nation's heartbeat - to reveal.

He was loved by lord and layman,
A people's poet so they said,
He rose to be Laureate,
Sovereign o'er the rest.

Dorene T McClure

OLD AGE
(OR A SENIOR CITIZEN'S LAMENT)

Wrinkle on wrinkle, crease upon crease, fold upon fold -
The knowledge: *I'm old!*
Yet how can this be? Inside I'm still *me*.
My eyes they still see - though not quite as well -
But my ears hear as well as ever they did.
My limbs have worn well - you really can't tell
When pain fills each joint - what's more to the point:
They still work!
The passion's there too, but really, in truth,
Belonging to Youth (They'd have us believe) -
Obscene in the old.
The one consolation was wisdom, I thought,
For are not the old supposed to be wise,
In spite of dulled hearing and dimming of eyes?
Yet though I keep waiting, and look for a sign,
This coveted blessing's not even yet mine;
And so I'll pretend, with good grace to grow old,
Like other old folk,
Yet all the time knowing my skin is a cloak,
My body a sham - *I know who I am!*

A Steele

A DOG'S LIFE

Three rings on the bell, all hell's let loose
It's Auntie Rona with the golden goose.
Biscuits galore - the sky's the limit,
All down my tummy in about a minute.
The kettle goes on - it's scrabble and tea,
And just about now I feel for a wee!
So I go to the door and give a good bark
Mum rushes out 'What's all this lark?'
She opens the door and throws me out,
And just for good luck she gives me a clout.
It's cold out here and getting quite dark,
I'd like to get in but I'm frightened to bark.
I think I'll leave home and move in next door,
I'll be welcome there and that's for sure.
No moans or groans or slaps on the bum
Rona loves me and she's not even my mum.
Well! I suppose it could be worse,
Take for instance poor old *Perc*
He's a Jack Russell - no friend of mine
Spends all his day on a washing line
He tears up and down from morning till night
I sometimes think he's not quite right
So when we meet on the field
I try to be kind -
What does he do - he bites my behind -
There's *no* justice in this dog's life of mine.

Simba

WINTER SUNDAYS

Raindrops racing along a window pane
Which one will be first!
Mesmerising, how one gobbles up another
And a single drop becomes a rivulet.
Take me back to wet winter Sundays
At home, a cosy fire, a lazy day
Playing games and singing songs
And me, watching
Raindrops racing along a window pane
Which one will be first!

Gillian Deas

POSSIBILITIES

It starts as a trickle
That's ever so little
Right up in the mountains so green
Then maybe starts flowing and growing and growing
But that much remains to be seen.
It may start going sideways
And flood all the highways
But no-one could know that for sure,
Then it may meander
With goose and with gander
And never stay dirtless and pure.
It may be stopped by a blockage
And rubble and rockage
And forever just stay there and dither;
It may never develop
Or grow and envelop
And never turn into a river.

Anna Williams

AUTUMN'S CAT WALK

Trees resplendent in vivid shades of yellows, golds and browns,
Dress now in autumn gowns,
The ladies appear to walk with straightened bow,
Reaching skywards once more,
Basking in the warm rays of the sun.
At last seeking no more to run,
But to revel in the thought of winter's dawning sleep.
Leaves already carpeting the ground disguising verge from road and curb.

Pleasure from God's thoughtful plan,
To plant trees to benefit man,
The air to oxygenate
For more life to generate.
Our souls to please
With utter ease
Oh fateful man where is your plan?

Frances Beet-Heaton

WINTER

The blue smoke curls from the chimneys
And loses itself in the soft grey mist;
While the fitful sunshine gleams
Like a smile so feeble it can't exist;
And in spite of the children's laughter gay,
The world seems a trifle sad today;

For it's shorn of its glory now,
And the leaves, and most of the flowers are dead,
And the mist in the distance grows,
And the last pale ray of the sun has fled.
Yet let the winds their vigil keep!
For this, seeming death, is the world asleep.

For the tired land must rest
Till it wakes again at the Kiss of Spring,
When the flowers bloom once more
And the buds unfold and the wild birds sing.
So leave the world to its well-earned rest,
And the mist that blots out the pale gold west.

Ann Brown

SCHOOL

Jimmy is a naughty boy he taught me how to swear.
I think he really likes me, yesterday he pulled my hair.
Andrew is a rotter he stood upon my toe.
Molly is a beast she really hates me so.
She pulled out my pigtails and pinched my behind.
You'll never be able to say she's lovely and kind.
Kirsty is so silly, she's always telling fibs.
Yesterday I laughed so much it really hurt my ribs.
I don't understand the teacher, I'm in trouble every day.
I try to get my sums right, I hate Maths anyway.
History is boring, cavemen and all that stuff.
Can't I leave school now, I've really had enough.
Geography is bestest, in English I am fine.
In just about three weeks time I'm going to be nine.
Nine is very old, I'm growing up so fast.
Can someone tell me how long school will last?
What are the alternatives, stay home and help my Mum.
Not likely. Mother hates housework it makes her glum.
I suppose I'll have to lump it, it can't go on for ever.
It does have its uses especially in wet weather.
When the sun is shining I want to go out and play.
I look forward to the summer holidays, I can play every day.

S Greenwood

FIELD OF SECRETS

Where seeds were laid into the soil
Green grass slowly began to grow,
Acres then turned into fields
And the peace of beauty of nature showed
The melody of birds in tune.
Animas came and made their tracks
Lovers made loving promises
To many of the questions asked.

Seasons pass as years come and go,
Still your green grass makes many beds.
Lovers adopt you as their field
In you they make their vows
And you are silent about what is said.
Yet sometimes promises are carelessly said
Tears fall heavily down upon your grass
You for them become a caring green bed
Still you say nothing of what is said,
In your silence you still remain sincere.

Secrets of love you will always have to keep,
Some being very good and some are bad.
Smiling vows on you have been made
Yet you still have sad tears in your bed.
From when love did sometimes stray
From promises made through the days.
These secrets are just for you to keep
In your field of green grass they will stay.

Phillip M Kesterton

THE SQUASH MATCH

Into the Arctic cavern the lions enter,
Whiteness envelops all-seeing eyes.
Thunder claps as the icy tomb is sealed.
Streaks of scarlet blood run from wall to wall.

Time is here, let battle commence.

The older lion full of guile,
The younger swift and strong.
Their prey the master of them both,
Though neither do no wrong.

Up above, the silent keeper watches,
Content to stand in safe confines,
Until the time should come to utter his
Unearthly cry
Of torment and torture to the lions below.

Time goes on, the battle flows.

Sabres slashing, silent, sure.
Cut and thrust of jagged edge.
Tormentilla's tireless tantrum
Crashes on to centre stage.

The lions they grow tired and weary,
The cavern's floor, no longer firm,
Melts slowly to a marsh of murky madness,
That shrouds the sun in dark despair.

Time has gone, the battle ends.

Older lion turns in triumph,
Sees the prey just lying there.
Younger lion, unbelieving,
Can do nought else but stand and stare.

Ken Williams

GET DOWN TO IT!

Tuesday is my keep fit night.
It makes me puff and gasp.
I'm sure when I am fit enough
The movements I shall grasp.

Why is it all the others,
When asked to stretch or sway
Follow one direction
While I face the other way?

I thought my legs were supple
And that I had some grace.
But it seems I have two iron hips
And a rhythm out of place!

Amongst all the other leotards,
Swinging legs and arms,
All I ever seem able to achieve
Are sweaty feet and palms!

Some make it look so easy
I therefore think they cheat.
I don't think their pulse rate quickens
As they get down to the beat!

Teresa Chatfield

PROPOSED ANTHOLOGY OF UNPUBLISHED POETRY

A virgin poet: that is me,
I write and burn; it's gone, you see.
A second glance at what first seemed good,
reveals the lines to be merely crude.

And so I cast them in the flame
and in a few days more I do the same.
My hobby makes the fire burn bright,
but others like them; and perhaps you might.

The world at large has been deprived too long,
of my epic works, in rhyme and in song.
The masses thirst, and why should they,
when it may be slaked by me; on a poorer day?

Why should my genius be hid from view,
when I can sent it in the post to you?
I wish you luck, and I wish you well,
and with me or not, I hope your book will sell.

Clement Boyd

DAFFODIL GAZING

As I roved out
By woods and lanes and dales
In clumps, by groves
'Neath walls and spreading tree
Along banks and shores
And motorway slopes in droves
Challenging the vivid-fire blossom
Of whin bush lee

Daffodilies' little heads
Everywhere a-bobbing up and down
Such pert little faces
Graceful limbs turned to the sun
A-nodding to each other
Hooray! Spring is truly here
And we'll don our best bright bonnets
For our season's a little one.

Caroline McCrea

THIS ANTRIM SKY

Feast your eyes on Bluebell Glen
The rolling hills with cow and hen
Thick bracken, gorse and leafy lane
Rainbows merging April rain
Swollen hilltops valleys blue
Wondrous beauty just for you.
This patchwork quilt I call my home
Forever aimlessly to roam
Through threaded fields of tangled wheat
To pastures new and village street
Where thatched old cottages abide
And tractor parts in long grass hide
A million flowers will live and die
Underneath this Antrim sky.

E Brown

JUST A KISS

If that's just a kiss
Then I'm the queen
If that's just a hug
Then I'm in a dream
If this is just sex
Then I'm green,
And I'm not green,
I'm in love with you.
Just a kiss from your cherry red lips
Just a sultry smile keeps me going a while
Just your body against mine makes everything fine
And it's always fine when I'm with you.
I hope our love keeps death at bay,
Just a kiss, has all this to say.

A M Denning

THE DOWNFALL OF HUMPTY

Humpty Dumpty sat on the wall
Humpty Dumpty was nobody's fall;;
With all the king's horses
And all the king's men
Humpty Dumpty took to his pen
He started to write to his local paper
A reply he hoped for sooner or later
Goosey Gander had borrowed his leathers
His excuse, was to hide his white feathers
Mary's pet lamb was covered in wool
All but one place, which showed off his tool
He told of the fun he had down the mill
With Jack's good friend, her name is Jill
He wrote it down about the pail
The things he could do with Jill in detail
They lay together in the corner
And who should walk in, but little Jack Horner
He grinned and smiled and said he would rough it
Introducing his girlfriend, her name was Miss Muffet.
It didn't turn to four in a bed
Jack forget to fill his pencil with lead
When little Miss Muffet spotted a spider
Humpty turned and said he would rider her
Three little mice came up from behind
Don't worry said Humpty, they're all blind
Humpty Dumpty exploited his mates
Causing a lot of squabbles and hates
Until the day police knocked on his wall
Excuse me sir, we've been asked to call
All his friends had met together
Humpty Dumpty had had it forever.

T Curtis

THE DANCING CONKER TREE

I saw a tree dancing to the wind this morning,
Reluctantly, I thought at first,
But the wind was in a playful mood.
So, she bowed her head and bade him do his worst,
And slowly she didst lift her arms
And waved them gracefully, first this way and then that.
But the wind said, 'Come along,
I know you can do better than that.'

And so she lifted up her skirts and flung them wide,
She danced and capered to the wind's strong tune.
Then, soon in wild abandon, she did shed her fruits
Of chestnuts. bouncing them along the ground.
At times 'twas like a ballet, so gracefully she moved,
And then again a whirling dervish she became.

At time quite uncontrolled he battered her about,
And then relented, and demonically held his breath.
So when at last she thought that she could rest,
Lowered her arms, proclaimed she'd danced enough,
The wind smiled to himself and said, 'She thinks I've don,'
So once again he blew, prepared to watch the fun.

Some of her skirts now tattered, she forlorn.
What started as a game became a fight,
And she of all her dignity was shorn,
And the wind just laughed and decided to take flight.

I saw tree majestic when I arose this morning.
My heart lifted at the lovely sight.
As she stood there gently swaying,
Having found composure in the night.
And I thought that life's like that,
As on a storm tossed sea, without a rudder
Or a sail, full of uncertainty.

Just when you feel that you can take no more,
You lift your arms and pray,
And he who sends both wind and rain
Enters your heart to say
Just call on me, relax, and wait,
You'll find tranquillity.

Kate Hobson

FIRE

Anne was up the stairs one day
Claire was watching tele
Smoke began to climb the stairs
It was really smelly

'What's that smell, what can it be?'
Claire has set fire to the new settee
The air was blue, Anne's face was red
'Claire you get up to your bed!'

'A bucket of water will cool it down,'
Anne said with a frown
Still in her night gown.

The windows opened wide
To let the smoke outside
When Steve found out
He could have cried.

The smoke alarm had done its job
As the sofa was a'frying
And the moral of this story is
Don't leave matches lying.

S R Masterson

KEEPING FIT IS FUN

I jog twice a week, six miles or more,
I start my stopwatch outside my door.
Running like made, I work up a sweat,
My breathing is heavy, my vest's all wet.
My legs are aching from thigh to toe,
I've still got over three miles to go.
Pacing myself, I slow down a bit,
As I'm passing people I try to look fit.
When safely past I slow down again,
Remembering the saying, no pain no gain.
I struggle to keep going, I've had enough,
Only one mile left, the going gets tough.
Finished at last, I tried my very best,
I go for a shower and change my vest.
Then I feel ill and lie down for a bit,
There's a great deal of fun in *keeping fit.*

Elaine O'Hanlon

EYE, SUFFOLK 1979

Eye! This sleepy little town you say,
'With railway gone the world has passed you by',
In isolation peace is found
And courtesy and care abound.
Polite the service in the store
Polite the customers, what more,
Can any ask for a little place
That seems to have dropped out of life's mad race?
House old and houses new
Some very lovely gardens too
A clean and tide town is Eye
I'm glad the world has passed you by.

Anne R Stratton

ROLL IN FIBREGLASS

You give me a rash all over
you make me itch, and squirm, and writhe.
You're like a disease caught from sinning
sometimes I wish you were just as curable.
Of course your society is pleasant,
knives in my back couldn't be better
or, perhaps I could say you
are a run barefoot on hay stubble?
Either one is beautiful.
Conversation is stimulating.
Grease on a newspaper, you ooze charm,
your jokes have more corn than flakes.
Compliments become snide remarks
that run from the edges of your mouth.
So you see, I do love you.
Come to me.
Let me embrace you, like a
roll in fibreglass.

Michaela Benson

WATER IS LIFE?

Starts at the top
Finishes at the bottom
Or is it the other way around?
Copper transport delivers the goods
But is it good?
Who knows what lies ahead
Or even past the next bend
Who cares or wishes to lend a hand
Does everybody bottle it up?
Is one drop spilled a waste?
Are tears just a drop in the ocean?

Neil Gould

TROUBLED

Troubled you are
Tired and pulled
Like the needle that's stuck at the seam
Drawn through rows of tangled knots
Reluctant
Where is the peace?

Trying you are
To clear the way
To that vision now blurred and confused
Seeking a path that is obstacle free
Vulnerable
Where is the peace?

Stifled you are
On a belligerent page
Ironing out line after line
Closing the chapter, speaking the verse
Unwilling
Where is the peace?

Strong as you are
And able it's true
To withstand all adversities of life
A determination second to none
Consistent
Where is the peace?

Continue, you will
To wrestle with persons
Always in your inevitable way
Consoling the weak, controlling the strong
Tolerant
Where is the peace?

Contented you'll be
When, you have stopped
Stepped off that relentless treadmill
Freedom, you need to capture the chance
Then,
You will find the peace!

Marilyn Roberts

FAIRGROUND RIDE (LIFE)

It starts, anticipation
People smiling, laughing
Spinning round and round
Minds confused for a second
By the laws of gravity and engineering combined

A rough patch, juddering
Screams of fear
Screams of excitement
Swaying backwards, then forwards
Faith needed for a second
That you'll make it to the end

Colours, flashing
Everything around you blurred
With the speed and pace everything is moving
So for a moment you close your eyes
Thinking of nothing but yourself
Then you feel you can carry on

Slowing down, near the end
A sadness, mixed with a happiness
Sad it shall soon be over
Happy you made your way through it
Memories of the scary moments
Memories of the happy moments

Simon Sinclair

THE TREES

I love to see the chestnut tree
How beautiful it stands
What a monarch it could be
To rule o'er all the lands
With its pale and candle flowers
It outshines all the rest
I could gaze at it for hours
The loveliest and best.
Just wander through a woodland path
And look around to see
The beauty all around you
In all its majesty
Don't take these things for granted
Enjoy them while you can
These trees have all been planted
For the benefit of man.

A Hendry

EARTH

Module One cruises out through space
With its crew on board, the human race.
The air filter system is being removed
By some of the crew to exchange for food.

The water storage areas are being polluted
As where to dump sewerage is disputed
The new power system creates toxic waste
Which we cannot handle due to our haste.

All life support systems are being abused
While limits on crew numbers are refused.
The question to be asked is I wonder why
We do this to our craft as in space we fly.

D J Williams

LOVE AND FRIENDSHIP

Joanne you are my greatest friend
And we've spent happy hours.
Without you dear my life would be
A garden without flowers.

At night I pray to God above
To help me on my way,
And find that road which leads to you
So there I'll know to stay.

If the world should end tomorrow
I wouldn't be alone
But if you're not here beside me
I couldn't face life on my own.

I'm not the best good looking fellow
You have ever seen
But deep inside there's a gentleman
Who'll treat you like a queen.

Of all the wishes that I ask
That would now complete my life.
When you will answer all my prayers
And one day be my wife.

So if these words don't touch your heart
There's no more I can do
Cause Joanne you mean the world to me
And I'll keep on loving you

Charlie McNeill

PAST RECOLLECTIONS

We all collect memories as we wander
        Down life's way
Some sad, some happy, some funny things that
        have happened, day by day
I've picked a few funny ones - I hope
        they make you smile
Life's too full of cares and woes - forget
        them for a while.

I've had a good life, but have had my
        ups and downs
Various strange and funny things I've done
        have caused many a laugh and a frown
Like putting soap in the fridge, and
        butter in a drawer
My daughter laughing her head off
        saying 'Mother' what on earth did you do that for!

I was in the ATS during the war and being short,
        on parade I had to lead the squad and try and walk tall.
Proudly I marched across the square
        waiting for the 'about turn' call
But to my horror, when it didn't come I marched on along and found
        myself right up against a very, very high wall
When a burly Sgt Major came up to me with his hands tucked in the top
        of his trousers, and below a massive tum
And said 'where the hell do you think you are going Tich - didn't you hear
        your Sgt's 'about turn' call!

I was striding through our local arcade
        on a rainy day
When over my shoulder a bedraggled smelly and dirty tramp -
        like an old man I saw
And thought - what is he following me for
        I began to get worried, what does he want with me?

But it wasn't until I stopped, the reason I could see,
      My curved brolly handle was in his pocket
So what else could the poor old man do
      but follow me - I stopped with many passers by
And laughed out loud - well wouldn't you?!

They say when getting old and senile
      you can do 'funny' things
So I'll have to watch my future antics
      Oh dear! What old age brings!

J Greenacre

LIFE

The implications that life beholds
Living, dying bought and sold,
The aged remember,
The young forget,
Husbands, wives, feeling regret,
Why are we born,
If just to die,
This earth,
This world of suicide,
This planet a game that we have created,
The people are players from this world of hatred,
If I lose,
I will die,
If I lose,
I will cry,
A false exterior being consumed,
By me, a human of death presumed,
Why do I try to change it all?
To change the minds of the world, how small!

Gareth Smith

BUSY TIME

Every morn when I'm on nights
I really do see some sights
I call my daughter at twenty past eight
Oh, please God, don't let her be late.

Putting life and limb at risk,
To catch the bus we must whisk
Eight thirty is it's departure time
For Stamford College, but that won't rhyme.

Hundreds of children all heading for class
'That one looks nice' - I think it's a lass!
'Watch out dad, keep your eyes to the front',
You nearly gave those cyclists a shunt.

'They shouldn't be riding five abreast'
'You shouldn't be looking at her chest,
Look! There's my friend just ahead
Drop me here dad, I'll walk instead'.

'I can't just stop then homeward bound
There's traffic everywhere all around
You'll see your friend on the bus
I don't know why all the fuss'.

Is that your bus just ahead
I really should be in bed,
It's over the crossroad and here we're stuck
Hasn't that chap in front got a right foot.

Your bus look, it's pulling out
Get out now and give a shout,
I'm sure I'm not, I'd feel a fool
With all those children going to school.

Run me to Stamford
Did you say
After all Dad,
You've got all day.

Peter Robert Leverseidge

THE PUDDLE SONG

It rains in Spain, we have no doubt
It does in Burgh Heath too
The weatherman's stopped shouting drought
Our lawn's a pond, that's true.

The February sky looks just like lead,
The wind's a roaring bluster,
Our hats are plastered on our heads,
The rain pours down the gutter.

What thoughts have we this soggy day
As we splash to buy the papers,
A chair, the sun, just sit and laze
Some golf or other capers?

We clean the house, scrape mud from floors
These trials we know don't last.
My spouse comes calling from outdoors
'Switch on the weather forecast.'

Phyllis Glanfield

THE PLANNER

'There is no wealth but life'
It says on a piece of my pottery.
Then why am I so anxious
To win the National Lottery?

I like to lie in bed you see
Planning how to spend a heap
It gives me far more pleasure
Than to count infernal sheep.

I do not plan a wardrobe
Full of fashionable clothes
Neither a freezer full of gourmet food
Nor cabinets full of booze.

I plan to fill my cupboards
All corners and all nooks
With videos and puzzles
Talking tapes and all good books.

I would generously also like to help,
The young folk of the town,
The Guides, Scouts, Twirlers, Football Teams
Others not yet noted down.

Buy more seats for the OAP'S
Placing some not in the sun.
Hire bands to play in the People's Park
A joy for everyone.

I'm sorry I can't ramble on
Of plans I've many more
It's time to switch the TV on,
Here comes another draw
          Ah well!

J Rudd

YOUR LIFE

Life is what you make it
And not what others say.
You don't have to stay up all night,
And pray within each day.

Do what you are best at,
And don't be led astray.
There's a time for everything
In work, rest and play.

Make the best out of what you see,
And go ahead and do your best.
Ignore remarks from enemies,
And protests from the rest.

If you take your guard down,
And let them get at you.
Think about who's going to be,
There to see you through.

Remember one thing though,
It doesn't count what others say
Just do your best to get up there,
And let the rest fade away.

Stacey Brown

HESITATION

Sometimes I think I ought to
And then I think I won't
But even if I could do
Invariably I don't.

Some days, I've really thought
I'd like to take this on
But if I'm too long pondering
The motivations often gone.

Some things really must be done
But if I pose the question, when?
I fret at the thought of doing it now
Knowing it could be done then.

Somehow, once I nearly did
Something that I shouldn't
But my conscience swung to right from wrong
And I knew very well I couldn't

Some ways I s'pose, it's rather sad
The way I hesitate
By missing opportunities
Indecision rules my fate.

Graham Miller

THE ROSE

From the smallest of seeds,
Which the gardener does sow,
Shoots a fountain of life,
In the earth down below.

Like an infant it grows,
From the dawn of each day,
Life and vitality,
Each leaf does display,

It reaches full bloom,
Each petal with beauty,
Strong against wind,
Protected from cruelty.

The seeds are dispersed,
Then slowly it dies,
Like an elderly person,
It's aged yet still fine.

As dusk sets in,
Its life has all gone,
But for a seed elsewhere,
There's a brand new dawn.

Lisa Forni

UNTITLED

If over nature I held sway
You'd walk in sunshine every day,
And everywhere your footsteps bear
Sweet fragrances would fill the air.
No storm or rain your path to mar
No stone strewn track your progress bar,
Dark cloud would melt and disappear
Before your presence, drawing near.
Grasses would bend before your feet
And gentle zephyr temper heat
Of summer sun upon the glade,
Tall trees would keep you in their shade,
And nature's beauty - calm - serene,
Be doubly beauteous where you've been.

Owen Jones

STARTING SCHOOL

In we go, through the heavy doors
Chaos, noise, shouts, first day that's the cause
They all seem to like it, unlike me
I've never been before, you see.

Mum said I'd get used to it
But I don't seem to like it, even one bit.
Too many faces, too much noise,
I'm led into a room full of toys,
Trying to be friendly now? Come, come.
All I want is my mum.

Where are you going, leaving me?
Just popping home for a cup of tea!
How can you do this to your little boy?
Haven't I always been your pride and joy?

Have I done something wrong to you
I don't like this school that's new,
Mum oh, mum please don't go,
I will behave now, you know.

She's gone and I'm all alone, here,
This lady's holding me, calling me dear,
She's not bad, I suppose,
She's someone I would have chose.

Bell's gone, I rush out,
Mum's standing there, I shout,
I've got lots of things to talk about,
I'll go back without a doubt!

S Dowling

THE SHOPPING ARCADE

The hum of shoppers, sparkling lights
at last the world is at its rights.
Some afternoon when mum's not tired
such happiness that is what's fired.

To huddle round in groups and chat
Tis gossip we're so sure of that
as groups all pass around their stories
from country farmers making forays.

Our cups are now so full of life
and money changing hands in rife
To turn the wheels of commerce round
let's try and not be too profound.

But spare a thought for all the others
The poor are still now all our brothers
Who have their rights we are quite sure
Let's help them now and be not a bore.

Their share of life they have a right
Let's pray for them with all our might
The world should be more happy now
so let's help them and that's a vow.

To share around the gifts of God
They were not made for just one 'bod'
That they will in the world be seen
and then the dove will go and preen.

G Evers

MY SISTER AND I

Two little girls you and me
Had our own special place up an apple tree
You had your bough, I had mine
There we would sit come rain or shine
Two little girls you and me
Most of the time happy and carefree,
But when you were sad then so was I,
Up our tree we would sit and cry.
I remember thinking as they cut down our tree
There was nowhere to go now for you and me
That tree had been like a second home
And now we would have to stand alone
Years rolled by - we grew up fast
But memories forever last.
You went your way, I went mine
No more would our arms entwine
No longer two little girls are we
Outgrown our youth like our apple tree
We both got married for better or worse
So here ended this little verse.
Before I go, I have one thing to say
Knowing what I know today
Life's not always been good to me
I should have stayed up that apple tree
If we go to Heaven, I'm sure there will be
A special place for you and me
If I go first, you know where I'll be
Waiting for you up an apple tree

Glenda Driver

68

TAKE MINE

The wind was blowing, bitter cold
As he pushed along the street,
It was raining hard and he was soaked
From his head down to his feet.

But he was wrapped against the cold
And he knew he'd always dry
His eyes looked up at the stormy clouds
In the dark and heavy sky.

He arrived at the little chapel at last
Within the hospital grounds,
The words of the doctor rang in his ears
But his faith, it knew no bounds.

The decision he now had to make
Was his baby or, his wife,
And whatever he told the doctor now
Was sure to cost a life.

So when he prayed, he begged the Lord
If you must have a life,
Why not take this one of mine
Spare my child and wife.

The doctor came to tell the man
Your son *and* wife are well,
The man just smiled, and breathed a sigh
A miracle? Who can tell?

Robert Marley

MY RAINBOW'S END

I saw a man cloaked in red,
He was standing high above my head
He said, 'Blessed are you for all you've done,
    You have followed me - the chosen one.
    I am the Son - the guiding light
    The epitomé of all that's right.
    I return for you in this night,
    Because you clung to me with all your might.

    No more in mortality shall ye roam,
    And soon my saint - I'll take you home.
    Back to that mansion in the sky,
    Home to your *father* who dwells most high.
    But 'til that day you will live in peace,
    And all the world their wars shall cease.
    Every knee and head bow,
    And confess me as the *Saviour* now.

    So look upon my wounds so deep,
    But do not sorrow and do not weep.
    I suffered thus that I may keep,
    All my blessed, faithful sheep.
    Rejoice at these wounds in me
    Through them you'll live eternally.
    You were more than worth all my pain,
    Because now together, for ever, we are again'.

I know my joy is now complete,
As I kneel down at His feet
I have found the treasure at my rainbow's end,
The most precious reward of all - my loving Heavenly friend.

Marianne Pilkington

DEMISE OF THE COPSE

On windy nights, awaking in close darkness
to hear the thunderous sound of
leaves, in masses swaying,
outside the window -
shaped behind closed lids.

Huge roars of leaves like mighty waves breaking,
heaving and mounting in great swells of clamour.
From such silent strength comes
so much motion.

On early summer morns
before humanity stirred
they would start, from leafy boughs,
in congregations - the birds.
A chorus of varied voices,
high-pitched, aching to break forth
in harmony and counterpoint.
A choir of nature's making.

A power-saw was all it took
to fell the growth of generations.
Stumps remain and only stumps,
where once beaked denizens
gave grace and joy
to branch and leaf.

The copse is no more.
Across the unprotected space where long it lay,
the leaves in winter gales no longer blow.
Now empty stillness reigns
within the darkened window
And silence, only silence.

Ian Hancock

IN CORNHAM WOOD

The snap of a twig betrays his return
To Cornham Wood on a winter's morn
The Saxon's leathery feet in the cold leaf mould
Trace invisible paths to his destiny
Destiny shaped by swords, seas and fire.

But now he has come back to reflect and die
On what he has brought to England
Brought it his sons and iron skills
From across the wilderness of raging oceans
Of another country he once inhabited.

Now, now in this very English forest still
With her musical brooks and cacophony of rooks
Amidst the bronze burnished floors of Cornham Wood
He sat down to muse on all things past
Muse silent on the immense secrets of his own world.

Through the cobwebs of hoar-frost
Spun sugary through the puzzle-bitten wind-filled trees
The old Saxon can now be seen
Resting his head against a blunt grey stone
His hands raised weakly to the leaden skies.

Time passes, he sleeps, he dreams, he dies
And when he wakes twilight had gathered him up
And taken him to the hallowed hall in the warrior skies
And so England, no the world is a little poorer for his departure.
Robbed now of this nameless Saxon.

Bequeathed us his sons, his sword and shield
Left us the answer to riddles he could never have known
Bestowed upon us his cast iron secrets
And left his name printed somewhere in the alphabet of stars
So that one day perhaps an astronomer may be able to give us his name.

Mark Asher

STORM PASSING: KESWICK

When becks are black against the snow
   And Grisedale blows his gale
And Derwent hurries to the sea
   Swollen in Borrowdale

When Keswick folk bend low to go
   From Bell Close to Main Street
Through ginnels where the whistling wind
   Near knocks them off their feet

Then in the night the sun inclines
   To kiss the coming day
To soothe the storm wind's agony
   And burn the clouds away

As a sweet bride in silken white
   A beauty in her prime
Dressed by her mother with a tear
   Upon her wedding time

So the sun gilds the golden day
   With ancient artistry
Lighting among the covered fields
   A glistening canopy
Tracing the curling snowdrift's edge
   Where the curved corries lie
Kindling great Skiddaw's snow-tipped crest
   Against an azure sky

On such a day while late we watched
   The shadows change we knew
That there's no art of brush or pen
   To paint the vision true

Norman Bridge

LISTEN

The glory of the mountains
The peaceful quiet dales
The silver moon, the sun's warm kiss
All these tell me - *God is.*

The sweetness of the flowers
The birds in happy song
The wind, the rain, the starry spheres
All these tell me - *God cares.*

The seasons down the ages
The autumn, summer, spring
The winter with its ice and snow
All this tells me - *God knows.*

The thunder and the lightning
The crashing waves at sea
Volcanoes with their deadly shower
Unite to tell me of *God's power.*

The butterfly so dainty
The breeze in leafy glade
The sunset bright with golden rays
All these show me *God's ways.*

But -   *The Saviour in the darkness*
        The thorns, the nails, the spear
        The terror of the cruel cross
        The silence, pain, the bitter loss
        Mocked by the crowds, bereft of friends
        Forsaken, dying all for me
        To think, He came from Heaven above
        Only this tells me. God is love.

E Barker

NEVER, NOT, NOR

Never tasted sweeter fruit
nor sailed through brighter harbours,
not walked on warmer shores.

Never called on such precious words
nor rested at ease with memories passed,
not ventured through the looking glass.

Never been too far from home
nor thought too much of letting go,
not a captive to the freedom flow.

Never gave the heart a chance
nor buckled under love's demands,
not wandered blind into the dance.

Never planned the perfect script
nor gambled on a lasting kiss,
not hunted out the hidden wish.

Never gave true love the space
nor entertained the sweet embrace,
not left fate to its willing ways

Never given chance the time to plan
nor taken time to understand,
not freed the lover in the man

Never
Not
Nor,
'til now.

W M Pearce

SHE WAITS

Little old lady with silver white hair,
sitting alone in her favourite chair,
Her mind full of memories of times now
gone, friends and loved ones all sadly
passed on.

She gazes across at an empty chair,
remembering her dear husband who once
sat there, her eyes fill with tears
her heart heavy with grief, her only
consolation that God willing he now is
at peace.

She sits waiting so very alone for
someone to visit or maybe just phone,
but nobody comes and nobody phones,
she just sits and feels pain from her
tired aching bones, with nothing to do
and nowhere to go time passes so very
slow the days seem so long and the nights
even longer, she eagerly awaits for the
day her heart beats no longer.

E Noyes

MY PATHWAY

Towards the end of my road is a pathway that speaks
to me,
The trees bow down to me,
and innocent birds sing a lullaby that is free.
At the end of that pathway is my destiny,
It is untouched and waiting for a new life to create
a better way of living.
Everything is overgrown and unchained to society's
clear, cruel misgivings.

This pathway has life
and I, a moment in its created freedom, am nothing
but a single moment of feelings.
I need its peculiar individuality to keep my
own sanity
to chase my own freedom.

Henrietta Barton

LAUNDERETTE

We sat in the launderette
and ate chips.
We stared at the open portholes,
the cabins all empty.
We rocked on the plastic seats,
orange and uncomfortable.
We laughed
and the emptiness was briefly filled.
You left and I remained sitting;
glowing in the window.
I glanced out at the street,
at the cars;
Stars shone from the headlights
and the road glistened.
I sat huddled in warm peach light:
outside it was cold.
Clear and crisp,
the air awoke me as you walked in
and we went out onto deserted streets,
our warm words froze.

Helen Norris

TORRENT

High on the mountain, whose peaks held supreme,
The magic of silence, lived a gay little stream,
That gurgled and laughed as it daintily sped,
Over glistening pebbles that lay on its bed.

And the little fish murmured 'We love you, please say
Just as you are, never leave us we pray'.
The little stream promised, did not comprehend,
Where there's a beginning there must be an end.

It laughed as it twisted and rippled along,
By the flowers nodding gaily, wee birds giving song,
To the joy of the children who sat on its banks,
To weave childhood dreams and to play childhood pranks.

Alas for our little stream, its cousins galore,
Joined in descent and soon with a roar,
It was caught in the whirl of a mad senseless race,
That gathered in fury and quickened in pace.

It was swept out to sea and cried in its fright,
As it struggled in vain 'gainst this mad useless fight,
Tidal waves, hurricanes, whilst all around,
Nothing but cold evil sharks to be found.

The thunder grew louder, blue skies turned to black,
A monstrous great bird screamed 'I'm alright Jack',
And then it was over, just a pitiful dream,
That beginning and end of our dear little stream.

Edmund Scott-Gurney

WHAT IS UTOPIA

In this consumer age, when the world is our stage.
False views, through the mist of uncertainty persist.
The disillusioned, hiss and boo, at whatever displeases them so.
      Is it Utopia they seek.

As electricity and transport are king, fossil fuel is the thing,
But plants have the power, because they must flower,
To grow oil, for engines to run . . . to be powerhouses of the sun.
      Might Utopia be mobility and speed.

When famine is our fate, because rain stops, or is late,
Plants never grow, because there's no water to flow.
As people pray for a shower . . . water is used to make electric power,
      Irrigation would be Utopia, so to speak.

When fossil fuel is too scarce by far, to use in bus, plane, or car,
A renewable fuel, a natural revolution, an alternative solution . . .
A seed of thought, to find new ways, to turn the tide on harder days.
      Would Utopia be a seed . . . ?

With our music cassettes, playing pop! As we make bets,
On horses that never run true, we must take the view,
Our world is in need, to recover from our greed . . .
      Then Utopia may start to exist!

Give me, by a mile, a laugh and a smile.
With sunny days that are warm,. with rainbows for charm.
Where caterpillars and frogs, have their place like cats and dogs.
      Utopia is bound up in mist . . . !

Jenny Major

THE WHEEL

Think of a wheel with bright spokes spinning;
There's neither end or marked beginning.
To each accomplished revolution -
Think of its gradual evolution
From wooden disc, its pace erratic
To tyred cushioned smooth pneumatic,
If slightly tardy in gyration
A minimum of lubrication
Will speed its fine rotating action
Geared and tuned to satisfaction.
Squat cars, sleek cars, long and narrow
Bikes and prams and garden barrow
Would all become defunct I fear
Without the ever vital sphere.
A wheel-less bus would be such folly
What price the supermarket trolley
Wheels of fortune, sometimes fated
Turning cartwheels when elated
Wagon wheels for travelling folk
Roulette wheels leave gamblers broke
There's food for thought with meals on wheels
Or steering ships on even keels
Cruising taxis, landing planes,
Round the world and back again
Arranged to keep the world's clocks ticking
Precisionally the cogs keep clicking
A simple ring of great potential
So common place, but how essential
Think of a wheel, a thought evokes
Could still be *nought* without its spokes.

M Morrow

SPREAD YOUR WINGS, LITTLE ANGEL AND FLY AWAY. . .

When I walked in I was amazed, it was so tiny. . .
White satin covered coffin, slightly grey around the edges.
It did not look new and clean
but already used, so lonely, alone, separated. . .

I felt their grief, cold like ice,
a sickly depression filled the air,
their grief touched me, people together, let down. . .

Filing out after the rain,
a thousand tears - nobody spoke, I felt their awful pain.

A chilly wind blew us to the little plot,
where many infants lay
some stillborn who had never seen the light of day.
She looked but did not see, he saw but did not look. . .

We waited awhile - hot tears, rolled down my cold nose.
A final prayer, stepping forward, looking in.
The hardest part for them.

Together we slipped in the mud, back onto the concrete path
and past the rubbish dump.
Where piles of rotting flowers lay scattered,
amongst ribbons and messages of love.

Her mother almost fainted, I kept talking, willing her along.
It was the saddest moment, when she finally spoke
'Where's my daughter?' was all she said. . .
I felt her drift away, to me she was lost.

I worried. . . they departed, she without a glance.
Her daughter came to me, arms outstretched. . .
I held her like my own
I whispered be strong, for one another,
and felt her sadness reach my heart,
right to the very bones.

Cora Tanner

THE MYTH OF THE FIRSTBORN

Firstborn

For a long time I have lived in the shadow of my non-existent elder brother.
They could not call me James (So it was Jacqueline instead)

They could not expect me to:
stack bales, castrate lambs, feed cows, drive tractors, muck out the byre
(All of which I did . . . and more besides)

They could not expect me to:
do well at school, go to university, earn a degree
(You guessed it! . . . I did it!)

They could not expect me to:
take over the family business, continue the family name, be their son
and heir.

How cruel society is to expect so much of my parents . . . and so little
of me!

Secondborn

And now I find that you also lived in the same shadow.
I thought you were the sun, the awaited one.
Is a tomboy not the same as a boy? I believed it was! Did you?

Thirdborn

Why so hard to picture you; my youngest sister?
Did you succeed where we two failed?
Yes! The daughter, accepted as a daughter.

Now I remember.
You were pretty, bright and bubbly, supple, feminine - all that we were not.

But look at you now - (you sold us out) fat and swearing, bearing sons.
Yet still the favoured one.

And finally the son

They did not like your name
But you must not feel bad . . . remember they wanted a son.
So Fraser you became - clan name, strong and proud. A *real* name for
a boy.

I think you suited Leslie better.

Lying here; calm, detached, almost unaffected I hope my sisters and my
brother can learn to smile at the cruel myth of first born sons!

Bhrighde

WHEN LIFE BECOMES A DREAM

As the sun takes the day to flight
The moon guides the stars to night
Escape
Images trailing behind closed eyes
Freedom from everyday ties
Escape
Reality broken and caged
Dreams free to be played
Passing
Echoes calling beyond my mind
Ebbing on a highway of dreams
Searching
Memories united with creation
Free from need of temptation
Rest
Our spirits are but dreams drifting
Within an eternity of imagination
Within

S Burst

MY SURPRISE

I know I'm getting on a bit
I do silly things at times
But what I like the best of all
Is making silly rhymes
Like the other night I went to bed
I found I couldn't sleep
So I wrote this little ditty
Instead of counting sheep
I know it sounds so funny
It's not even worth a prize
But I'm going to call my effort
My lovely big surprise'
It happened one day in the summer
The weather was lovely and calm
When all at once I thought I felt
Someone touch my arm
I wasn't frightened
There were lots of people around
But when I tried to walk away
My feet wouldn't touch the ground
And as I stood there shaking
My body feeling quite numb
I heard a voice call from behind
It's only your old mum

V Mosley

LEAVE ME IN OR CLOSE THE DOOR

Our love is so new,
so new that I wonder if it's love at all,
yet you give me that sinking feeling,
that I'm heading for a fall.

One minute I feel so proud,
to be right by your side,
but at other times, unknowingly
you make me just want to go and hide.

I get the impression you want me,
but your feelings you'd rather me not see,
at times you want to be near,
but getting too close is what you fear.

You've been hurt before, and maybe that's what pulls you away?
But you have to wake up to reality, that you could love again someday,
so either leave me in or close the door,
so should I move closer, or walk away for evermore?

John Ridd

THE WEEPING WILLOW

Weep for the weeping willow.
Down in the dip, by the evergreen ponds.
Scarred with 'Tizer' tins, and nameless rubble.
They have felled it today
All that remains, a few lonely logs.
Why have they done this?
Only yesterday, I sketched that very tree.
Every year it heralded the first blush of spring
A hazy pastel green.
Who gave the order for this sad execution?
Down in the dip
Weep for the weeping willow.

Joseph Stocks

FULL CIRCLE

They said that we were far too young and yes
      perhaps we were
But pride was hot and love was strong
      and our days looked set fair
We tumbled headlong into love without
      thought for rhyme or reason
Why should we worry, today is ours
      never mind the month or season
Never mind that pennies were all we
      had and not very many of those
We had each other and we were rich
      for that was the life we chose.
But life has a way of making us pay
      for pleasures which we crave
And as years go on we begin to learn
      we must obey the rules and behave
We must grow up, we must learn
      respect, we must do our duty with care
And soon we learn that life is good
      and we will all get our share.
We learn to have patience and cherish our fortune
      If fortune we are destined to find
And we learn to share our good fortune
      With all the rest of mankind.
And as we grow older we come to know
      We don't really know much at all
We marvel at the luck we've had, that we
      Survived. We didn't fall.
Well, yes perhaps we were too young
      But love has seen us through the trials
And hopes the failures and fears
      Our love still prospered and grew.

And now we have come to that happy state
        When we sit back and our blessings we number.
And we'll be young again as we finally
        Sink to that beautiful peaceful slumber.

Ruth Newson

DARA

Lying by a blazing fire
Glowing on a winter's night
Stillness - quietness,
Not a sound -
except
for the crackling of the embers
and the contented murmuring of
the dog.
Jet black, she is -
But for the white tinges on her paws
Soft and warm
to touch.
Suddenly -
An excited twitch in her body
Is she awake?
No
A lick of the lips
Chasing a rabbit - perhaps,
Now, quivering eyes
As if straining -
To find it
Until,
Unnoticed
She stops - as it it was never there.

Blair R Forrest

COMPREHENSIVE

I'm scared to go but my friends are excited,
They think they'll be delighted.
Easy maths, easy english, they mumble amongst themselves.
All I think is hard maths, hard english, when will this fear go away.
As time flies by the day is getting nearer.
Will I enjoy it, will I dread it.
I wish I was an infant again playing in the sand, doing what I
wanted, painting, drawing, chatting to my friends.
No homework, no stress, no depression.
Oh why? Oh Why do I have to grow up so quick?
The next thing I know I'll be looking for a job.
I used to be playing Mob but now I'm walking round the yard,
lonely as can be.
Nobody talks to me.
We had a leaving disco yesterday, but I don't want to leave I'm
happy where I am.
I'm used to one hundred children about twelve in each class,
but now the numbers multiply in each and every class.
With just one week to go, what am I to do?
The uniform's so big and fluffy.
Skirts, trousers, tights, socks, shirts, ties, new faces, new
people, new names.
The worst part of all will be if I get lost, who will I turn
to? where will I go?
Oh well, I can't stop clock's from ticking or the seasons
passing by.
I'll just have to wait, and hope.

Natasha Ferguson (11)

CLOUD TEN MORNING AFTER

I feel different today
I don't look any different
Maybe a little happier
There is a spring in my step
My hair seems shinier
I see myself reflected in shop windows
I even smile at myself
There is someone who matters
He told me I do
I never believed it before
But I believe him
I love him where I can't love myself
I can still feel his arms
His breath on my face
If I close my eyes I'm with him again
I'm in love with the world
I want to embrace everyone
I see couples together and I'm happy
I'm one of them
I share something with them
No longer cold in isolation.

I don't think it meant this to him
He loved me last night - but now
If I see him with someone else I will not cry
I will not hate him
For one night and one day I'm happy
He lent me happiness
I feel different today.

Sophie Rogers (17)

LOVE

What is love without a kiss?
What are feelings without expression?
For no couple's love can be the same,
Nor can we explain our emotions,
We simply define our bond with a word
But it is more;
Love is infinite,
And as a result, so are we.

R Cotterill

WINTER

When the whooper swans fly in calling
like the hounds of heaven on high
The wind keens in from the arctic
and there is no one here but I,
As the dawning light grows stronger
and I wait for the sun to arise
The marsh is clean, frost-dusted
fresh to the human eye.

I accept the solitary figures
that in this landscape blend,
Wildfowlers and bait diggers
whose way 'cross marshes wends
Such, like the swans, are transient
yet each one has his place,
Their ancient occupations
have not changed their pace.
So, silently I will paint them
against a sunrise sky
And should you chance to see me
- At a distance pass me by!

Andrew Church

THE MAN OF WAR

The Man of War stood alone
On the battlefield not far from his home
Chemical weapons had been used.
His shin was burning, his feet bruised.
The Angel from heaven came down
A golden light shone around.

The mask upon his face was tight
He tried to remove it with all his might
The Angel with gentle wings
Took him to heaven in early spring.

Anita Massey

NATURE'S REMEMBRANCE

The clouds are racing with the wind
Interrupting the sun's bright light
Light rain falls like gentle touch
Why am I so still?

The scent of the flowers in May
Fills my mind with memories past
Petals cascade and dance around me
Why am I so still?

The blackbird sings his morning song
Welcoming day like a new dawn
Nature stains and colours my soul
Since my love has gone.

Steve Filby

A TRIBUTE

Pay tribute to the working man,
Who from birth to old age,
Or what're life's span.
No privileged place,
For him you see,
From hand to mouth
His succour be.

And there's the woman
By his side.
Who tries to make
A goodly life.
That all may share
The worldly prize,
Of happiness in children's eyes.

For they who wear the purple cloak,
Have never felt the worker's yoke.
It's always been beyond their ken,
To understand the working men.

God loves the common folk the best;
Made more of them than all the rest.
Pay tribute to the man and wife;
Who live as best they can their life.

God's blessing on the likes of thee,
The ordinary family.

Windsor Hopkins

JIM RETIRES

This world the day is aa gan wrang fin ye hae a good look roon,
I'm sure in twenty years or so, there'll nae be tradesmen in the toon.
So dinna think yer time's been wasted, dinna think it's been in vain,
Wi the kind o wirk that's deen the day, hooses winna be the same.

When yer wirkin days have clean run oot, noo dinna sit an greet,
Pit aa yet tools up on the shelf, sit doon pit up yer feet.
Bit dinna sit for ower lang, for it's nae quid for the body,
Jist hae a think on fit tae dee and find yersel a hobby.

I widnae recommend the drinkin, it be a gie expensive wye,
Although wie some folk noo a days, it seems to be the cry.
The game o golf is nae sae bad bit I ken it's nae for you,
And I've tried the game of bowls masel, an I'm dammed if they'll run true.

Some days ye'll hae time on yer hands, so think aboot yet wishes,
And turn yer hand tae your quid wife and help her wie the dishes.
I ken that she's been quid tae you in a the years geen by,
And though hoosework's nae yer style, ye could aye geet a try.

Fit ever ye wid like tae dee, an I'm sure ye'll hae been schemin,
And if ye'd like tae live a while, then forget aboot the weemen.
So my advice tae you wid be, just dinna be a feel,
And find yersel a jobbie like the eens ye dee sae weel.

We wish ye a the very best and hae a fling the night,
There's naething like a wee bit dram for a guid auld fassioned vright.
So look ahead on times tae come and never mind the wither,
And some night nae sae far awa we'll hae a dram thegither.

Sandy Donald

PRIVATE DANCER

The girl on the bridge stands aloof and
Alone. Her wind whipped hair
Flying streamers in the mist;
Breeze blown dress
Waving cotton flags in the dusk.

Whispering boughs of
Beckoning trees, dismiss the sun
With a hurrying tone -
Call the approaching dark
With rustling murmurs.

Birdsong dies while movement comes alive
In a waking waltz of the nocturnal.
Leaves spiral in a petticoat swirl down
To the paws of the genteel fox
In his hunter's coat of rust.

Owlish eyes light the night
And the swinging, swaying bridge
With its solitary dancer.

Rag doll limbs on a tumbling weight
Screaming silence welcomes
The lake's applause.

Marie-francoise De-Saint Quirin

PRESELI HILLS

Sweeping green and purple hills
The sunlight on the hollows
Clouds that race across the skies
Making shadows follow.

Breezes in the gorse bush.
The grass, an unnamed green.
The springing moss the sheep keep cut,
The sparkling chilly stream.

Snowdrops, daffs and bright blue bells
All mixed with stones of blue,
A quarry pit with water deep,
Of a real unusual hue.

The seasons change, the beauty stays,
Deep in the country's belly
The greatest joy one can receive,
To walk in the Hills of Preseli.

Sue Canny

WHAT'S IN A NAME

If dandelions were scarce as diamonds and pearls,
You'd find them in borders of barons and earls,
Let it be known they're toilsome to grow,
And their stand will be crowded at Chelsea Flower Show.
Ladies would vie, their bonnets to grace
As they paraded at Ascot - and lost at each race!
Bride's would look great as they walked up the aisle
The bouquet would take pride of place for the 'smile!'

We grownups regard these flowers with scorn
As they're thought to defile a beautiful lawn
But a toddler will crawl, gurgling with fun,
To clutch what he thinks the fairies have done!
When next you go out, your garden to mow,
Remember their maker - he designed them, you know!

Roy Nercombe

LIFELINE

His long term companion
Was a faithful cocker spaniel
Hand licks,
Knee cap sniffs
Licking toes through sandals,
A swishing tail
That wags away
Whenever his lead is jangled,
Two large, brown eyes
That mesmerise,
If ever he's mishandled.

His loving, devoted wife
Had lately lost her life,
With no curable answer
To the power of cancer
She was cruelly sacrificed,
Her husband suffered
The withdrawal of her loving
On which he readily relied,
The strain of his loss
And a broken heart
Were more than justified.

The routine he contrived
Was designed to occupy his time,
Therapeutic thoughts
During longer dog walks
Tranquillised his mind,
Paw shakes
Eased the heartache,
They even made him smile,
His canine friend
Proved a blessing
Making life worthwhile.

Glenn R Lumb

CHILDREN OF TOMORROW

Children of tomorrow
What planet will they see
Full of toxic poisons
No longer blue and green.

If the day should ever come
That greed can be suppressed
Will the planet have enough time
To save itself from death.

Poisons in our rivers
Flowing to the seas
Soon all the fish will be dying
Full of mutations and disease.

What will be left of the forest
As we chop down all the trees
A bleak and barren desert
Shall be our only legacy.

The politicians give speeches
Full of empty rhetoric
Cowering below big business
Who might see their profits slip.

We must stand up for the planet
The rain forests of Brazil
The Rhino in Africa
We must no longer let its blood be spilt.

Don't let me stand alone
When I give my battle cry
Or the tears of our children
Will mark well our passing by.

D Carthy

HOCK

Here I am, my lifes's in a muddle
It's not too bad, but a bit of a struggle.
We've got no cheques, we've got no cash
We'll have to give life another bash.
We play Bingo, we play the pools
We've not much luck, we must be fools.
She's sick now and resting in bed
The pains real bad, it's all in the head.
You will be strong and healthy you will see
You will be telling me, what will be, will be.
The shopping is done and put away
Only one problem, how will we pay?
The cheques like rubber and will bounce away.
The mortgage and bills haven't been paid
The bailiffs are outside ready to raid.
They break down the door with their big axe
Don't worry wife, just sit and relax,
They can't take the table, it will only break
They can't take the paintings for they are all fake
The stereo's broke and so is the TV
It's no good mate, you'll have to take me.
It won't be easy, I ain't got much clout
Six month's of porridge and I'll be out
The wife came to visit every now and then
I'll tell you wot' mate
          Never Again!

James Royle Jnr

FROG IN A BOG

Down in the depths of a smelly, squishy bog
Lived a rather noisy, green and grumpy frog,
He burped and he gulped and he croaked all day
Hopping about in a splishy, sploshy way.

Froggy stuck out his tongue and splat went a fly
Then he crunched and he munched and swallowed with a sigh
You would think he'd be happy in his muddy, slimy niche
With bugs, grubs, flies and worms well within his reach.

But Froggy was a foreman of a fishy factory
And snails, slugs and slow-worms made his life a misery.
Everyday there was a riot on the grimly, grimy shore,
'No oxygen, no work!' all the protesters swore.

There were pickets in the pond weed
The fish turned in their fins
The roach went on the rampage
Sardines cringed in their tins.

'Our population has exploded,
No air, no food, no sun',
So Froggy solved their problem. . .
And ate them. Every one!

Belinda Hastie

THE GARDEN OF DELIGHT

Come and see a conammara garden
It's a source of infinite delight
Turn to the right
In a mixture of greys
In a mixture of greens
The blend with the wall
And surrounding scene
Is the place
Where Pat makes the bricks
To the left of the gate
In a tree sheltered place
Is a quaint built house
Of a bygone age
There is no sound of voice
No steps on the stair
Because you see
Its the hens
Who live there
Follow the wall
On down the field
It's dressed in abstract pattern
With next winter peat
To a big fishing boat
Stretched at its ease
Amid daisies and buttercups
Hens and geese
And on a still summers day
There the lap of the sea.
The high crying of birds

The humming of bees
Little blue genatins
Play hide and seek
And wild, wild orchids
Stand tall and free
In a conammara garden
Down near the sea.

E Armstrong

LOGS TO THE MILL

Timber is God's gift to man
So why on earth
Do we exploit, the deforestation
So eagerly sought,
By man's greed,
So cheaply bought,
A thousand years to grow a tree
Five minutes with chain saw
Goodbye to thee.
A once leafed-filled glade
Alas no more
Trees have gone for evermore
No songbirds sing, to the human's delight
Only motorway madness
Keeps us awake at night.
O Lord hear our prayer
No more felling
No more yelling
Show us the way
To a better living.
So we can prevent
Our Earth from decaying.

Gordon Dangerfield

OLD BESS

The Welsh sheep dog trials were beginning
In the usual way, more or less
But this year old Dai attended
Along with his faithful dog Bess

The course was extremely exacting
The judging exceptionally keen
And Bess, with her ears sharp and twitching
Was alert as she ever had been

From the moment Dai started to whistle
Bess took the flock firmly in hand
Shepherding, left right and forward
Obeying Dai's every command.

She held them in check whilst she deftly
Guided each through the gate in the pen
Her performance, which could not be faulted
Earned a maximum ten out of ten

As they both received congratulations
And the crowd gave a heart-warming cheer
Old Dai stood there proudly and told them
That Bess had been trained just by ear

As the judges had watched her performance
With never a sheep left behind
Not one of them ever suspected
That Bess, all her life, had been blind.

Nancy Calladine

NORFOLK LIFE

It's nice to live in Norfolk
The Broads and waterways
Where boats they just glide along
And spend some happy days

With woodlands and the wild life
And open country side
With pleasure of the country lanes
If you go out for a ride.

You'll see a few old windmills
Where most are standing still
You then see one a working
Which gave us quite a thrill.

You'll see them country cottages
A pump stands on the green
It is a bit of heritage
And always to be seen

The village shop keeps busy
It sells most anything
From bread and milk and papers
Or biscuits in a tin

Next time you come to Norfolk
And have a lovely time
Remember us old country folk
That Norfolk home is mine.

B Salter

CHRISTMAS

Christmas is a happy time of year
Holiday for all at Christmastime
Reindeer pull the sleigh of presents,
Ill will is forgiven.
St Nicholas is Santa in this day and age,
The tree covered in tinsel of all colours.
Musical carols go on through the night.
A Saturday morning is the Christmas Day
Snow falls as Christmas comes.

Gordon Millar

WHEN WE WERE YOUNG - NOW FIFTY YEARS ON

When we were young and lithe of limb
Come eighteen, thought we were men
We heard out country's clarion call
Mortgaged our youth for the clamour of war
Though not your brave knights, in armour bright
We fed on the exuberance of life
Sought the happy comradie of clubs and pubs
And sometimes we thought of higher things
When danger threatened, we were scared
Beset by fear, our souls were bared.
'Did you have a good war' they said
We often thought, Thank God, we are not dead
And prayed for peace, and our own homestead.

Norman Mason

THIS IS YOUR LIFE

O, please dear Michael, never put that book into my hand,
If you knew what I've got to hide, I think you'd understand.
It all began when I was born, you can't go back no farther
It's true I had a lovely mum, but no dad to call my father.
I couldn't wait to leave school and get meself a job,
Working in a chip-shop, not bad for thirty bob.

The more you have, the more you want - and I wanted more money,
I got an office job at last, but that wasn't so funny.
I palled up with a chap there, posh suits and lots of dash,
But the meals and drinks he bought me came out of petty cash.

Swing back the curtain, Michael, bring on the guy called Sid,
His wife found out, he paid me off - with a hundred quid.
Here comes old Mrs Dangerfield, she really was a caution,
Bled me half to death, she did, after my first abortion.

At least my husband won't be here - 'cos he passed on last May,
Stabbed by the boy he left me for - 'cos he was gay that way.
O, they could find a thousand people that I've met and knew,
But to find one who would come tonight - there would be very few.

So to save a lot of blushes, and perhaps domestic strife,
Please dear Michael, never say - 'Dear June, This is Your Life'.

June Rees

THE SHELTERS CAN'T PROTECT US NOW

The skies turn black, reflecting the void in my mind,
Surrender to destruction, of all mankind.
Here the ultimate killer, tilting calm to hysteria
One button, switch on nightmares, we cower, defenceless, inferior.
Mushrooming cloud implodes, a frenzied pandemonium,
Fall out reigns over a playground for plutonium.
The blistering air explodes in dying pleas,
The stench of scorched flesh, a torn civilisation,
A suicidal world through mans own creation.
Where once a proud building, now hunches a gutted black shell,
Where once a living being, the memory of his tortured
                    scream, now marks where he fell.
A promised land, turned to wasteland, sighs a shrouded breath,
Where the regal join the ragged on their knees to beg for death.
None survive the holocaust, here failure prevails,
Death has no prejudice, it has no social scales.
The life, the smile, wiped from our planet's face,
A triumph for humanity?
A step towards insanity?
The earth became history,
Goodbye a trivial race.

Sue Butcher

MY UNSEEN COMPANION

Nose so cool and silky
Velvet to the touch,
Friend of smoothest satin
To feel, to stroke, to clutch.

You are my unseen freedom
With me throughout the day
A home, love, food and friendship
Are all I have to pay.

Through the dark street guiding
You never do complain
I was in desperation
And then along you came.

Although I cannot see you
I know you in my heart
My wonderful companion
We'll never be apart.

Charmaine Bird (12)

MY HEARTTHROB

As a part time pools collector
Going from call to call
I meet all sorts of women
Married ones, most of all.

But one particular lady
Uppermost in my mind,
Is a real fantastic raver,
But she's also very kind.

To meet her is a pleasure,
One of the 'perks' of my job,
And there's no doubt about it,
She has become my heart throb.

We've agreed to get married,
And settle down for life,
But there's just one small problem,
I can't get rid of my wife!

J Bayford

FRED

Fred's mum and dad had drunk a lot of beer,
When they changed their name by deed-poll
to a month of the year.
They may have been eccentric, but they raised him well
for he is humble, moral, kind and funny - just as well.
I was told in 'The Fox and Hounds' by Lucy's friend Ken
that Fred had spiked the drinks of some blood sportsmen.
They swore that they'd get revenge, which made me feel sober,
I must sabotage the hunt for Fred October.

Philip Beavis

THE CHOP

I am a little fir tree
Sitting in the snow
What am I thinking?
Whose home am I to go

Will I go to a nice one
Like the one before me
Where there were Christmas
Carols sung around the tree.

Festooned in coloured fairy lights
With an Angel on the top
Dressed in white netting, but
Oh, how her wings did flop.

I'd better stop now -
Here comes the chop.

Nancy Sharp

COLOUR

Only the beautiful can hold colour in their palms;
Can nurture it like a mythical bird
Or nurse it like a wounded beast.
Only they can sing the songs unheard.
Only they can press Venus to their beating breast
With here mercury waste cradled in their alien arms.

Only the beautiful can live as love commands;
Without the need to search for what lies beyond
The veil of velvet cloud separating the child from heaven.
They know peace in Venus' tender bond.
Behind their eyes the prettiest colours remain hidden,
Like impossible birds in distant lands.

Luke O'Hanlon

GOING TO THE VET

Off they marched me down to the Vet
To look at the lump on my neck I bet,
It wasn't causing a lot of pain,
But it did look nasty now and again.

On Sunday however, the damn thing bust
So now an operation was a must,
I had the op and felt quite woozy,
Have to go back again next Tuesday

I'm glad it's all over and I'm feeling fine,
I won't get worried when I go next time,
So my friend please don't fret
It's not so bad seeing the Vet.

S Page

DARLING, I LOVE YOU

Darling, God has yet to create the flowers
that would express, my love for you.

If I were Leonardo Da Vinci
your portrait, would bring us both fame
if I could write lyric, like Gershwin
inspiration would spring from your name.

But all I can say is I love you
it's been said so often before
darling, when I say I love you
I wish that I could say more.

It was easy for Shakespeare and Byron
it's poetry just watching you walk
if I could write music like Mozart
I could catch every note as you talk.

But portraits, poetry and lyrics
have left little for lovers to say
darling, when I say I love you
what's left for a lover to say.

Hugh McCallum

THE DOLE (TO THE SICK)

I'm still on the dole, my head's completely blank,
Over three and a half million already sank.
My biscuit is crumbling, but what can I do
They've offered me jobs, but only a few

I'd sign on every fortnight, it made me so sad.
A second rate citizen alone and in rags.
I'd travel the streets, looking for work,
And when I'd get home at night it really hurts.

The children bedraggled, hand me downs on their backs.
They sleep huddled together not knowing the facts.
My father was a miner, he worked very hard,
Mother buttered his bread with the scrapings of lard.

He fought for his country the children and wife.
All six they brought up on the edge of a knife.
For me there's no future, but what can you do?
Cause you can't look for work
With only one shoe.

Steven Bennett Whiteley

ALONE

In deep solitude in solace alone;
I bring my fears to the Master's Throne.
And when my heart is heavy and sore;
I kneel and pray, I need no more.
And I have passage through the Cross;
I will not fear or suffer loss.
My Saviour, my Master, my Healer, my Friend;
My riches, my glory, my world without end.
My deliverer, my confessor and my life;
My port in a storm and earth's strife.
I'm never alone, He reminds me each night;
I'm doubly yoked, my burden is light.
For my burdens He lifts, my way He makes straight;
And I no longer trust luck or believe in fate.
And in all my ways I trust to Him;
He has give me life and taken my sin.
So don't despair or suffer alone;
Kneel at the cross and He'll bring you home.

Leslie James White

CHORES

I was so disorganised my house was in a state
To be all clean and tidy would make me feel just great

So after giving this a lot of thought I made a resolution
I'm sure with effort, I could find the right solution.

I would get up very early and make my beds, all three
Get a lovely breakfast and a nice hot cup of tea.

I would polish, vacuum, sweep and clean
I would bit my tongue, uttering nothing mean.

The children would be organised and be as good as gold,
Not answering back, not acting up, doing exactly as they're told.

My hair would be brushed, my clothes would be smart
My washing all dry, due to my early start.

I would clean up my kitchen and make it all shine
The rest of the day was bound to be mine.

I would read, knit and sew, design a new hat,
Play with the dog and cuddle the cat.

Sit in the sun and get a good tan
Cook a nice lunch, not eat from a can.

All of these things would fill me with glee,
To spend so much time just being me.

But then in the morning I awoke with a start
My spirits had dipped and I had lost heart.

I gazed at the clock, already passed nine
I would have got organised, but I hadn't the time.

Jean Hinton

THE DAFFODIL

I look out of my window, the air is cold and still
The sweet song of the robin is clear and shrill.
No grass can be seen either day or night,
For all around is a sparkling diamond white.
Underneath the snowy ground laying snug and tight,
Life is waiting to burst forth when the time is right.

The snow is thawing the sun doth shine,
The aroma of Spring smells so fine.
My eyes survey that patch of ground
And there before me a shoot I have found.
Green and strong its life begins,
And now the skylark sings.

From shoot to stem and a blaze of yellow,
The colours of spring are warm and mellow.
In the blink of an eye the Spring is past,
The flower before me is dying fast.
The bloom is wilting it's growing old,
The green grass turning a burnished gold.

The leaves are falling all around,
Spreading a carpet upon the ground.
The clouds have come where the sun once shone
A tear in my eye the flower has gone.
That patch of ground is again white and still,
I'll have to wait until next Spring to see my daffodil.

L G Montgomery

A DAY IN THE LIFE OF A SCHOOL SECRETARY

Before I've got my coat off the phone begins to ring
It's Mrs Smith, about her son who's sick and won't be in.

It's 9 o'clock, the kids in class, now parents are at my door
'We want to see the Head', this means trouble, I'm sure.

The Head has left a list of jobs, 'Is this for today or for the week?'
With so many interruptions, you'll be lucky I say (tongue in cheek).

The phone has run incessantly, feel like taking it off the hook,
So I can do the dinner registers and give the numbers to the cook.

Right now I'm going to open the post, Oh, a child has come in late
'I've just been to the dentists', the post will have to wait.

I'm going to get some work done now, I've just sat down and then,
'Can you make some coffee please, I've got visitors at ten!'

It's 10.30 time for a break, for a well earned cup of tea
As I start to take a sip - 'Can you come, Sarah's hurt her knee'.

Help, can you come at once the photocopier is stuck
I pull the offending paper out and get covered in oil, just my luck!

Back at the office a parent wants to give me some money
To pay for photos, trips and dinners, this really isn't funny!

Now Fred has just thrown up and Jimmy's had a fall
Bang goes another dinner break, must give their parents a call.

Will it be a quiet afternoon, I really don't think so
Now here comes a salesman, so I tell him where to go!

There is no money left at all, we've teachers salaries to pay
So I just gently put him off, 'Come back next year, I say'.

It's nearly time for the children to leave as mums start to drift in
And complain 'My child has lost his coat!', 'Have you looked in the lost
property bin?'

The day is always busy, but there's one thing I like to see
Someone coming in to say, 'Would you like a cup of tea?'

It's 4pm, I'm going now and I haven't done a thing
Never mind there's always tomorrow, I'll go before the phone starts to ring.

Sheila Chapman

AUTUMN REFLECTIONS

The lovely blooms of Springtime, all too quickly fade and die,
But the memory of their beauty, lives on in one's mind's eye.
As with all the lovely memories, just waiting there, in store,
To brighten up the dark hours, and bring out the sun once more.
Every life has its darker moments, when we are unhappy, ill or sad,
But looking at the wider picture, good times far exceed the bad.

Memory, like a photo album, holds pictures from our past,
And a half forgotten song, or scent, takes us winging back there, fast.
Through scenes remembered from our childhood, the dark days of the war,
To family gatherings, weddings, happy holidays, and so many more.
A kaleidoscope of memories, each one special, in its way,
Our minds' diary of the life we've lived, from childhood, till today.
And unlike photographs and souvenirs, which we may lose, or treasure,
They won't fade or tarnish, they will stay with us forever.

So though old age is creeping on, there is still so much to do,
No time to sit and vegetate, some dreams can still come true.
I'll enjoy what each day has to offer, take my chances whilst I may,
And store up future memories, live life to the full each day.
Though we can't see into the future, life can still be great,
I'll enjoy the beauty all around, and leave the rest to fate!

Kathleen Adams

SUPERMODEL

She stares straight ahead,
No tracings of a vain smile
or grateful recognition that she's here.
Steel blue eyes, lips set in plaster.
The chocolate coloured streaks on her milky skin
appear natural in the harsh unflattering light.
Blood red nail polish
reminds her of some distant scent. . .
Sherbet and cyanide.
Finally the performance.
The gold slinky gown slips from her silky shoulders
falls in a pool at her china doll feet.
She offers herself to an audience aghast.
The frenzied flash of abruptly awakened cameras
capture the only beauty that is ever
natural.
Supermodel.
She turns on her dove soft heels
and saunters back, loose-hipped,
in rewind motion.
Necks crane.
Her gas blue eyes dance.
Supermodel is alive.
Supermodel could keel over in the wings
but for now -
now the naked charm is captured and conserved,
She's alive.

It lasts all of thirty seconds.

Sarai Robinson

116

THAT PAIN - OR WOMAN AWOKE
FROM ANAESTHETIC DURING CAESAREAN

Blast to cast-ice numbness by a sudden draught,
I left in glass display to journey home.
No sound, no consolation needed (Car radio placed
Grating textures, ugly on my blank-walled seamless fall)
But one chord struck quick before I switched;

She spoke of waking into hitherland of
Numb awareness, voices first, sang joy:
'. . . baby's weight. . . ' the endless tunnel through!
Heavy months anticipation released her loved anew.

But swift as love a searing hurt became
Alive from where her joy had lain, deep seated
Screaming signals tore and pulled in pulses,
Rose bursting on the surface of her brain.

Her leaden body dead to all communication.
Slight echoes from that cave of torture found escape.
They saw in panicked horror, minute flinches sent
By every wrench upon her raw and open womb.

In hope and prayer, found drugs to pacify,
Alleviate and numb, (but best laid plans become
More terrible than unmade others when reversed),
Failed to reinstate her sleep: continued work undone.

On writing her report for trial,
Eight pages of verbose protest flowed
'Til need to term in words, the pain, arose.
But no word in the language came.

So quietly and finally I left. . . though
Cuts that tore in untold sorrow still remain.
But only silence will suffice
A certain type of pain.

Tola McKellar

ALL ALONE

Little old man,
On an old park bench,
Who years ago,
Fought in a trench

What did you fight for,
If this is your home,
What did you fight for,
If you're all alone,

You fought for freedom,
You fought for power,
You fought for life,
That's born each hour

You fought for the bad
As well as the good
Someone should help you,
If only they would

But to them you're a tramp
A man they once knew
All of us owe freedom,
To someone like you

Bev Gay

THE WITCHES

The witches are out on their broomsticks,
Round homes the witches fly
High and low around the sky.
The children are playing,
The witches frighten them,
The children run away.
The witches laugh and laugh again!
The witches fly away.
Z Wilson

118

FOREVER GREEN MY VALLEY NOW

Forever green my valley now,
Forever green and still.
The wheels are stopped from turning now,
And ne'er they ever will.

The shambling queue of men is gone,
The ponies put to grass.
No more to tally one by one
As through the gate they pass.

The sound of voices raise in song,
From choirs that still remain.
Though competition's just as strong,
The 'hwyl' is not the same.

Forever green my valley now,
No more the clouds of dust.
The trams all stand in silence now,
Forever left to rust.

Silicosis sounds out loud,
Through air that now is clear.
Its fingers grasped both weak and proud,
And cost some families dear.

The throb of valley life has gone,
No neighbours call as yet.
Both man and wife stay home alone,
To wait the coming debt.

Forever green my valley now,
They've closed the doors to hell.
Forever poor my valley now,
They took the jobs as well.

Neil Shedden

GETTING MARRIED

The strangest feeling
Couldn't describe
The way I'd felt
For years inside

Could've been love,
Never be sure
Listened to him,
There was no cure

Never met him,
Heard his voice,
Wrote to him
Without a choice

A radio show
Was all he had
And a life of his own
Drove me mad

After 6 months
He replied
Felt some hope
From deep inside

Meet him maybe?
Where and why?
But he'll be married
In July

Luckily now the
Feelings have faded
Met someone better
He's been down-graded.

Emma Jones

TEDDY

Teddy staring from one sightless eye
You never laugh, you never cry,
Through all my childhood tears and joy
You've witnessed me, a growing boy.

You're ragged now, all bald and torn,
You've been with me since I was born
When we were new, when we were young
With all our best songs to be sung.

Now life has torn both you and me
Sadness weighs so heavily
When I get sad, when I get blue
I sit awhile and think of you

Life is a game, we've played it well
I've walked, I've run, sometimes I fell
But looking back I still recall
When you were new and I was small.

Michael Champion

KING

Welcome night people, to my humble abode
I'm sure you recognise me from tales of old
Once I had kingdoms, glory and gold
Now I have nothing, or so I am told.

I am the King of the Night, of darkness and dreams,
I'll tear your illusions apart at the seams
All is dissident in my world of mystery
Come with me people, come with me.

James Morrison

COUNTRY HEART

I was bred and born a country lad
North beyond the Boston fens
Sometimes in this life of mine
I wish I was back there once again
But if I was to go back
I think I would feel sad.
And reminisce too much about
The good times I had there as a lad.
Places change and people move
Things don't stay the same
But my hearts still in the country
Looking for open spaces.
Of all the farming land around.
And longing just to hear.
All the country sounds again
Like the crowing of a cockerel.
As he struts among the hens.
I picture a little old country cottage
Somewhere north beyond the Boston fens
With roses round the door
And some chickens in a pen
New laid eggs for breakfast
With all the country sounds again
But would I be contented
Just like I used to be
Or would I just grow old without
The lady of my dreams

R Atkin

122

AT READING RAILWAY STATION

An old man wanders down the subway
Staggering alone on this VE day
Where he goes we do not know
On and on the rivers flow.

This old man with a tearful manner
Sickle and hammer, Star Spangled Banner
Swastika, Union Jack, Rising Sun
A falling bomb, a firing gun.

This old man walks far, far away
To departing steam trains of a distant day
To girlfriends waving, to kisses goodbye
To aching hearts and fearful eyes.

With ghosts of friends all at his side
Laughter and drinking that has long since died
With ageing heart that is forever young
In the eyes of his grandchild, this fathers' son.

An old man wanders down the subway
Staggering alone on this VE day
An angry group of boys appear
Chanting a song and drinking beer.

Gareth Harvey

THE HERON

Silent motionless sentinel
Neatly clad in grey and white
Yellow eyes, alert and bright,
Stands in the river shallows.

Rod straight, the scaly legs
And feet resist the water chill,
Poised the body, intent and still,
Awaiting Nature's bounty.

The bayonet beak, pointed, keen,
Stabs through the surface of the stream!
Flashing gold in the sunset's beam,
Droplets fall, glistening bright.

The heron rises on graceful wings,
Beating the air in measured flight,
Into the dusk of oncoming night,
Home to mate and nestlings.

Mary Baillie

UNTITLED

My past has been happy and clear
We had a tremendous love together
You dispersed my loneliness and fear
I thought we might make it forever.

My present is incredible hurt and pain,
The best aspect of my life has fallen apart,
If only I, or we could be the same,
But I must learn from the pain and treat my heart.

My future is uncertain, I am afraid
I need someone, you were ideal
But I will never forget the words you said,
And you will never know exactly how I feel.

Although this is the end
I wish it was the beginning
I want our hearts to mend
So that love can keep on winning.

Chris Boddy

UNTITLED

I dreamt as I slept in the old armchair,
Of the flock of geese, winging through the air,
The swans on the river, with their artistic flair,
And the foal in the paddock, beside the chestnut mare.
The old oak tree by the seasons worn,
Where I'd sit as a lad and blow my horn,
My best Sunday clothes all tattered and torn,
Hair like the army lads, shaven and shorn.
The embers in the grate on a winter's night
Wrapped in a blanket, tucked up tight,
Peering into shadows, with the candle light,
Snow against the windows, a beautiful sight.
The fingers of old age creep up on me,
But I shut my eyes and wait to see
The pictures of my life as it used to be
A boy then a man, responsible yet free.

Sally Tyler

UNTITLED

War and decadence, lies,
the end is hidden inside
as the unknown soldier lays down to die
His trusted helm split by the force of a word
Cold lips mouth apologies
traitorous thoughts thrash wildly in the last throes of death
For now he belongs to no army
fights for no cause
and as his body gradually returns to the earth
the ignorant and the blind rush to take his place
and to follow in his glorious footsteps.

Dean Callaghan

MARSHALLING YARD

Long gliding apprehension waits in the dark,
Wondering what wares await transportation.
Cold bands of steel rest on wooden sleepers,
With regimental gauge and plexus of points.
The twittering of dawn releases the pregnant
Potential of night's twinkling expectancy.

Flaring, a match shoo's away gloomy shadows
And sends sulphurous plumes skyward.
Warmth creeps along the footplates heart,
Whilst shuffling shoes - 'tap and crunch, tap and crunch'
Long lines of rolling stock, sounding out safety;
The trucks keen to collect their cargo.

Orders from above float down the line
And ally on a clipboard.
Chuffing smoke and steam, the shunter dovetails
A queue of multiple mutterings for manufacture or sale;
Designated destinations invoke images of
Sombre work shop or shimmering white shelves.

Flag and whistle invite a bird's eye view,
Down upon the yards yakker, where a
Punctuated pageant of carriages and carts
Tankers and trucks gather on parallel tracks.
'Clitter clatter, chitter chatter,' the power pulls
Slowly at first, but gaining pace now.
Till at last the thundering wheels signal
The passing of a train down the tracks of my mind.

David Machin

LOSS OF MEMORY

Where am I going
What is my name
Can anyone tell me
Am I to blame?
People surround me
But I can't recollect
I feel so alone now
With no self respect,
Can anyone tell me
If I have any kin
It seems there is
Something,
That's locked up within
My legs are so weak
Now,
My body feels numb
I just keep on walking
In the heat of the sun
I see a white car with
A lovely blue band,
A lady in uniform is taking
Me by the hand,
Come along love your looking
All in,
I'm taking you home and back
To your kin.

Jean Worsfold

LADY P

You're a pool of Perriers'
in this dirty desert of a world,
and you're a piece of fresh tomato
in a British Rail sandwich, all curled,
and Lord I wish you were mine.

Your a Stradivarius,
in a down-town punk band,
and you are one song,
that will never be banned,
and Lord I wish you were mine,
for if I was with you,
I wouldn't care if the sun don't shine.

You're the last greengage apple
in a nuclear holocaust
and if I was running for my life,
for you I would have paused,
and Lord I wish you were mine,
for if I was with you,
I wouldn't care if the sun don't shine,
for with you,
any weather would be fine.

I'd run full pelt,
North, south, east or west,
in the pouring rain,
in just my pants and vest,
with a deadly python,
gripped tight round my chest,
if you,
were the object of the quest,
and Lord, Oh I wish you were mine.

Doctor Blade

LUCKY

He lay so still, there was no sound
A ball of fur on the ground
Bleeding and sore, no pads on his feet
He'd walked for miles in the summer heat
No food or friends for at least 10 days
Taken for a fox, in the sun's haze.
His coat was terribly matted.
Hadn't seen a brush or comb
Surely someone missed him
When he never returned home.
But he had been abandoned, well
That's what we were told.
Fancy being turned out of your home
And only six years old
We nursed him back to health again
He never made a fuss
We knew in our heart, he would have
Died if it hadn't been for us.
Such a lovely collie, faithful through
And through. We're very proud to own
Him, we think you would be too.
We've called our dog 'Lucky'
An appropriate name you see
One day perhaps you'll meet him
Then we think you would agree.

S Buckingham

JEALOUSY

So she dances, moves with the motion of a gale
Swirling within me,
Turning with anger -
Tempest!
Lightning in her walk
Such spite in her talk
Her hair burns hot red
Like the fire in my head.
She stands there, so surely,
Such horror of beauty
'Just one look now, baby'-
Just one look could kill.
Burn! They say,
But they never knew
The power of that anger
Or force of her rage.
Yet I know this fire
For I am its slave.

Beth Watts (17)

PROMISES

Don't promise me you'll love me always
How can you tell?
Life is for now, not mortgaged to tomorrow
And promises are frail
Transient as bubbles drifting on the wind
Or Jack o' Lantern light
Luring one on
To flounder in a slough of love denied.

I dare not ask that you should love me always
No one can tell
Love's not made prisoner by promises
It must be free
To find another love if this one fades
And life goes on.
So love me now
For in the end all promises are vain.

Eileen Forrest

FROM LITTLE TO BIG

There I stood open mouthed
Tears in my eyes, I looked surprised!
For here is my little girl dressed all in blue
I thought this can't be true, my little girl's no longer there.

Alone I must leave her
To school she must go
I hope she does well
I stand and wave
Tears in my little girl's eyes
As she disappears.

Her first day has ended
The doors fly open.
Out she runs straight into my arms
For here is my new big girl
The little one no longer there.

Andrea Reid

131

GOODBYE 25

It was a bitter tongue that called herself savage
Lying in the road like a piece of sharpened glass
Sowing stones in the field to reap stones
To sow stones;
And the gone are forgotten for the sake of the going
And the dead are forgotten for the sake of the dying
Did no one save the silenced music
And does that river still flow?

This conflict is as old as me, older still,
I know the names of the streets and the lanes and hills
And I never came closer than a picture on the news
Or a scar on the hand of a visiting soldier.
Do I then have a right to speak in turn
To raise a dark pen and stab at virgin paper?

This letter bomb war
Has been fought without words
When now, it seems, words have made all the difference
I lost the plot so long ago
I'm left believing in blood from stones.

Twenty-five years makes a bitter cake
But if memory will stay but let tomorrow pass
Then a bell may sound out a simple cry
For a loss, for a cry to the gone and fast
And a long cold winter;
Goodbye 25
I have heard that river whisper:
Alive, Alive!

Charles Tinniswood

ABJECTION

He covers his head
His arms enfold him
He shuts out the world
Holding a world inside him.
His eyes uncomprehending,
See endless change and utter confusion.
Who are these people who proffer help?
Where is the care of his mother and father?
All gone, all gone, all torn apart.
No war, no drought, nor even abject poverty
Have turned his world into a frightening desert
'Tis one which is mainly of his parents making.
Who are we who struggle to reach
And give a helping hand?
Only he knows the total misery,
We cannot see or properly understand.
Outsiders' help is but a ripple on his gloom of sand.
Indeed, we can add to his confusion.
We do not fit his life's perception.
No wonder he turns with snaps and snarls,
No wonder he lacks zest for school and life.
For what has life been as yet?
The future holds nothing as far as he can see.
No wonder he knows not how to love or care
For those who should have loved and cared
Are so very often just not there.

Patricia Willgrass Holmes

THE BATTLE OF BRITAIN

Cleaving the blue dome of Heaven
Scaling, scalene,
Shades of the ghost of Grenville
Intrepid, keen-eyed, desperate,
Fur-coated, grim-lipped,
They fought.

They tore the Hun invader from the sky
The tiny aerial ships
Wove patterns of pure silver in the sharp blue air,
Amid the bomb laden bellies of Armada galleons.
Drake smiled. His bearded lips
Spitfire.

Zooming. Up and up and up and up,
A wild crescendo of shrieking engines,
The scream of straining metal,
And the sudden anti-climax
As they rolled and fell, spitting a leaden stream of death
Upon the black invader.

Far, far, below, half hidden in the mists of morning
The Towers of London,
And at intervals a tongue of flame, flared and licked upward
Like a match-head marking a bomb mark
And the depths spewed up from belching muzzles
Paths of death.

They fought and fought and fought
Internecine.
Dead they are deathless
Dying they live,
And we live too
In consequence.

Bill Tame

I LIE ON MY BED

I lie on my bed, watching TV
The news comes on with pictures to see,
Bosnian pictures of horror and pain,
My God, all that misery, what do they gain,
Death, destruction murder and rape,
I turn over the channel, so that I can escape.

Escape from the sights, of the Bosnian war,
Switching the channel, I see United they score,
Strange how the world is, it's not really fair
For some it's only death, destruction, despair.

I switch back over a child's been made blind,
Those doing the maiming, don't they bloody mind,
One day it will have to end, once and for all.,
The old Yugoslavia will be peaceful, no more children will fall,
But until then, I'll just watch some of the news,
Then getting upset, turn over, for the soccer pundits' views.

Will it be United or Villa, to add to the score?
To take my mind off, what the news showed before
My God, I am lucky that I live right here
Not like others, shivering, cowering, living in fear.

Robert H Griffiths

THE AIR RAID

When the siren, starts to blow
To the shelters we all go
Food, flasks and books galore,
As the guns begin to roar.

Overhead the bombers drone,
In the streets lie bodies prone,
Air raid wardens, whistles blowing,
People's faces, fear showing.

In the refuge far below,
People huddle, row by row,
Gas masks hanging at the ready,
Children clutching favourite teddy.

Once again the bombs explode,
'Hope that wasn't in our Road'
Someone shouts to Mr Morgan
'Will you play your old mouth organ?'

Soon we're singing loud and clear,
Trying hard to show no fear,
Vicar says 'Shall we now pray'
Soon t'will be another day.

Finally the siren wails
Everybody moves like snails
Picking up their treasured gear
Thanking God for the all clear.

John Parry Booth

NEPTUNE'S KINGDOM

Oh! To stand upon the beach
Be it winter or summer's day
To feel the wind upon my cheek
And taste the salty spray -
To hear the seagulls'
     Plaintive cry,
As they feed along the shore
And white horses canter by -
'Neptune's Kingdom' to explore.

But oh! To be upon the sea,
And hear the billows roar
This earth would Utopia be -
I'd ask for nothing more.

And when my sojourn on earth is ore'
Please heed my humble plea -
Take my ashes to the shore
And cast them in the sea.

White horses then I will ride
And content forever be
For on each incoming tide
I'll travel wild and free.

Matthew Cosby

NO GREEN OR BLUE

Sod Haig and all the General Staff
Sod the Colonel and the major too
Sod the Captain and the officers of the line
The Sergeant, Corporals and all their blasted crew
Now no longer is there green or blue
But only bloody red
And out there some God damned mother's son
Waits for me to raise my head
Just one thousand yards of churning burning earth
His world and mine
And those great yawning chasms scream silently
Don't worry lads, you'll all be mine in time.
You'll see no more green or blue, my boys
But just that bloody red
And just one thousand yards of burning earth
Before the bastard shoots you dead.

Brian Potter

TRAPPED!

I sit alone watching nothing,
Seeing all, but do not care;
People pass by, no one sees me -
Why is the world so unfair?

In my world nothing is wasted,
(None of 'them' care if I'm dead)
I do my best just to survive,
A cardboard box for a bed.

Bins are the only friends I have -
They feed and clothe me each day,
In them I find all the things I need,
Things that most folk throw away.

I can't go on living the way I do
But how can I break this chain?
As soon as I pick myself out of the dirt,
I fall straight back down again.

Julie Gillespie

PLAYING WITH FIRE

Deep, deep in my heart
Did the flame of love start
Now it burns day and night
Memories still keep it alight
I know I can never be with him,
But in my head I still hear him
You see the flame in my soul,
Is from a love I once stole.

Every once in a while
I wake up and I smile
Behind conscience's laws,
That flame of love roams.
A law I cannot avoid.
Or our lives are destroyed.
You see the fire in my soul,
If from a love that I stole.

They said if I played with fire,
Then I was a fool and a liar,
But when I lit the match
I was so sure of my catch
Now I'll never be with him
Tho' my spirit cries out for him,
You see that flame in my soul,
Belongs to a man I once stole.

Marianne Kennedy

BURGLARY - A MESSAGE TO MUM

Dear Mum, to what can I say? I sit here on this sad, sad day,
Your call did really touch my heart, so sad we live those miles apart,
I can do nowt to put things right, but put my thoughts in verse tonight,
Someone entered your home within, so committing a mortal sin.

To you the things that you hold dear, should so suddenly disappear,
No money can these things replace, or put that smile upon your face,
Your home and castle been betrayed, for justice to 'Our Lord' I prayed,
Not for vengeance that is his, whether it be mister or miss.

All our lives you've loved and given, can we ask to be forgiven?
That such a thing should happen to you, when all you do is love us true,
I write this from your son and daughter, no I don't want legal slaughter,
All I want for you today, is not your life in disarray.

Just the mother we know and love, sent to us from Heaven above,
So strong for us when things go wrong, without you how'd we get along,
Your life goes on no matter what, their jealous of the things you've got.
A family who loves you true, always there to stand by you.

To those who went in mother's house, your life will be just cat and mouse,
A life of crime just doesn't pay, it may happen to you one day,
Sit and think how you might feel, you'd not believe it to be real,
So if you have a conscience voice, *No more stealing*, that's your choice.

Pamela Simms

I WROTE TO HER IN JULY

I wrote to her in July
Another day passes no reply
Mind amiss with sensuous bliss,
Through lingering reminiscence,
Of her kiss.

Each new night I prayed for strength
I loathed the way she didn't call,
My endless desires my pointless soul,
I yearned for her Rock n' Roll
But I lived to see jealousy unhinge
Where all my tears had made me cold.

There is no cure for a dead feeling,
No cure for love's unhealing
A street like any other,
Just a simple girl,
With an ordinary brother,
Just a kiss,
That fatal bliss,
And love that lasts forever.

Gareth Nixon

BUST

Lurching forward through the night
In this hazy roaring coffin of excess,
Without another's lips
To feed my self importance.

In my slow reflections,
The wide moment of the night
Becomes a disappointment,
Becomes a waste.

For all I did was dive
Into golden ignorance,
And tomorrow, or today -
Come aches and clouds.

I glance around with piercing eyes,
Trying to divine the happy souls;
Trying to divine -
Myself
Lurching forward through the night
We must return to what is right.

Declan Lawn

A WIFE'S LOVE

My love I give to you freely,
No charge or reward required,
My love I give to you without question
No strings or conditions applied.

My love I give to you only,
To my husband from his wife,
My love is yours to cherish
And should never be denied.

My love grows as time passes,
Our memories we begin to build,
With bricks of different colours,
My love will be fulfilled.

My love will be with you always
From now till the end of time,
Love me forever,
My love, my darling,
Mine.

Correna Vickers

ALONE

There I was, just standing there,
looking down at the big colourful valley beneath me.
I could taste the freshness of the air, it was
cold fresh, it almost hurt to breath it in.
I was very high up and everything was still,
just sitting there as if time had stopped.
I had my dogs with me and they also were
Standing there looking down, as if hypnotised.
Their noses were sniffing, they were standing very
straight with their tails slowly moving from
Side to side and their ears cocked. . . listening.
It was wonderful up there, I was in a trance,
looking down at the beautiful colours of autumn
Gold, green, red, orange, yellow, beautiful bold
colours blending in with the rich green colour
of the different fields.
A couple of seagulls broke the silence
with their cawing noise and flapping wings
then, silence.

Kelly Simpson

MODESTY

My intelligence astounds me;
I'm a genius through and through.
I'm also very gifted
And it's absolutely true
That though you think me boastful
And exceptionally vain,
There are not many mortals
Who have such a splendid brain.

When inspiration strikes me
As a flash of brilliant light,
I put my pen to paper
And then proceed to write
The poems which flow so smoothly
And I really don't know why
My peers are so frustrated
That I never need to try.

At sports I am outstanding;
I hurdle, jump and run.
They require so little effort,
That I do them just for fun.
My musical ability
Is lauded far and near -
If I wasn't so preoccupied
I'd make it my career.

It's certain I'm extraordin'ry
And improving every day.
I'm truly quite proficient
In each distinctive way.
My siblings think I'm haughty,
My 'friends' say I'm aloof,
But I cannot help my prowess
And this poem is my proof!

Carolyn Bell

144